HOMESCHOOLING
AND
LOVING IT!

12210 Herdal Dr. Suite 11
Auburn, CA
95603
Editor@Homeschool.com
Printed in U.S.A.

ISBN: **978-0-9816171-2-1**

Cover Design by David McNutt
Page Design by Julie Jenkins Sathe
Editor: Aricia Lee

Praise for *Homeschooling and Loving It!*

"How many parents, upon embarking on their homeschool adventure, ask their children 'What do you want?' 'What is important to you?' More often the pressing questions are 'What does the state want; what's important for college?' The message in Homeschooling & Loving It is so terribly important because it encourages parents to ask life-changing questions of their children; questions that, if they will really listen to their answers, will actually help them discover their dreams, and find God's purpose for putting them here on earth."

Barb Shelton; *author of Senior High: A Home-Designed Form+U+la (www.HomeschoolOasis.com)*

"I'm loving Homeschooling and Loving It! It is well-written, well-designed, and much needed! It clearly and simply starts at the beginning and shows the way to the end. It takes into account more than "school" and goes on to incorporate all aspects of learning, but most important, it revolves around discovering and encouraging each child's uniqueness and individuality. Whether you are new to the idea or homeschooling or just need to regain momentum or change directions, you'll find this book most helpful. Step by step it guides you to think, design and gather the resources to carry out a homeschooling plan that you and your family can not only live with, but thrive with. Your biggest disappointment may be, like mine, when you come to the end and there is no more!"

Joyce Herzog, *author, speaker, consultant www.joyceherzog.info*

"I've read many books on homeschooling, and this one is perhaps the most user-friendly on the market. Each chapter progresses logically and is packed with valuable information. And to make that information accessible, each chapter includes a "Suggestion Box" with advice from veterans, plus a recommended family activity. Homeschooling and Loving It! wins a 10 out of 10 for practicality and inspiration."

Rhonda Barfield, *author of Real-Life Homeschooling: The Stories of 21Families Who Teach Their Children at Home*

More... Praise For *Homeschooling and Loving It!*

"Homeschooling is one of the most important choices a family will ever make. While the decision should be based on research and information, the daily routine of it needs to be based on a mutual passion for discovery, ongoing respect for each other and the joy that learning as a family can bring. With Rebecca's book in hand it will be easy--and so worthwhile!"

Tamra Orr, *author of "Asking Questions, Finding Answers: A Parent's Guide to Homeschooling" and "America's Best Colleges for B Students."*

"This book is a gem in every aspect – one of the best homeschooling books we have read. Filled with practical advice and warm wisdom, Rebecca can help you make sure that your homeschooling is joyful and comes from the heart."

Win and Bill Sweet, *Authors of "Living Joyfully With Children"*

"As the homeschooling wave continues to gather force in the U.S. and around the world, Rebecca Kochenderfer has been at the forefront as a facilitator, educator and cheerleader. This truly wonderful book is a comprehensive and interactive approach that will help any parent--from the seasoned veteran to the wary beginner--to clarify personal vision, approach and structure. A parent who follows Rebecca's guide will almost certainly find success and fulfillment in the homeschool journey. Heartily recommended!"

Oliver DeMille, *President of George Wythe College and author, "A Thomas Jefferson Education, Educating a Generation of Leaders for the Twenty-first Century"*

"From cradle to college, Homeschooling and Loving It! covers just about all there is to know and do in order to love homeschooling. Newcomers will get off to a great start in their homeschooling, and veterans will learn new things that can add joy and inspiration to their days. Rebecca Kochenderfer's informative and encouraging writing style lifts and supports rather than piles on guilt. Her activities at the end of each chapter help the reader put "legs" to their new knowledge, making this a very useful family workbook for all family members. Homeschooling and Loving It! strikes a delightful balance in attainable "structure for a purpose" while moving yourself and your children to life goals. Even non-homeschoolers would benefit from this practical and helpful advice for family living."

Marilyn Rockett, *author of Homeschooling at the Speed of Life*

More... Praise For *Homeschooling and Loving It!*

"The best way to turn your **children** into **self-learners** is to get them excited about learning, and one of the best ways I know to get your **children** excited about learning is to follow the advice in *Homeschooling and Loving It*."

"Joanne Calderwood, Educational Coach, Speaker, Author of "I'm the Mom; I Don't Have to Know Calculus / A Self-Teaching Manual"

"Rebecca has done it again! Who wouldn't want to homeschool after reading this book? Practical and inspiring, Homeschooling & Loving It! belongs in every parent's library, even those who are not homeschooling."

Mariaemma Willis, co-author Discover Your Child's Learning Style and A Self-Portrait(tm) Learning Style Profile, www.learningsuccessinstitute.com

"This book will become one of your most treasured resources. The information on goal-setting is so valuable it can change the course of your child's life."

Pat Wyman, founder of HowToLearn.com and author of "Learning vs. Testing"

"I wholeheartedly recommend 'Homeschooling and Loving It.' Whether you are a beginner or an experienced homeschooler, this book will help you build a stronger and more loving relationship with your child."

Martin and Jenifer Thomas, co-authors of "Slice of Heaven-a family on the move" and parents of five homeschooled children.

This book is dedicated to my wonderful homeschooling guinea-pigs …
my children:
David, Christina and Madison.

And to my wonderful husband, Bill.
Thanks guys for loving and supporting me.

How did I ever get so lucky?

I also dedicate this book to our incredible
Homeschool.com Product Testers. Thank you for answering all those
surveys and sending in your suggestions. I love the way that
homeschoolers are always looking after each other.

And for you, Aunt Dorothy.
You are greatly missed.

TABLE OF CONTENTS

FOREWORD

By Marilyn Mosley Gordanier
Founder/Director, Laurel Springs School

Homeschooling and Loving It is all about celebration, staying inspired, touching your sense of purpose, and having fun.

Thank goodness that homeschooling is "an idea whose time has come," and there's a road map which allows its expanding number of parents to comfortably see homeschooling as one of their options. Rebecca Kochenderfer's heartwarming book, *Homeschooling and Loving It*, gives parents the support, information, and tools to demystify homeschooling and make it a very workable educational option.

Thank goodness for *www.homeschool.com*, a virtual gathering spot where all kinds of homeschoolers can meet and explore information from the varied and rich forms of home study. *Homeschooling and Loving It* combines inspiration, purpose, strategy, and the tools needed to take on the magnificent job of educating your own child. This must-read book answers key questions such as: What is homeschooling? Is it right for me? Will my child be able to get into college? Could I be a great homeschooler? What are the benefits of homeschooling? What about socialization?

It was a warm October day in 1981, when I embarked on one of the greatest journeys of my life; homeschooling my youngest child. This momentous occasion was not triggered by a serious problem at school. In fact, my son had a lovely teacher, and the school was a small country schoolhouse, with one class per grade, set in the midst of orange orchards and palms trees. But it was very clear that my son was not happy and this form of education was not the best possible option for him. In fact, by the age of six, he had gone from being excited about school to waking each morning tired, cranky, and saying he wanted to stay home with me. Our first year of homeschooling was blissful, just the two of us working on story books, math problems, saving baby birds, art projects, and taking trips to the Natural History Museum in Santa Barbara. This was the beginning of an epic journey that would change my life. Soon, his older brother and sister were eager to try homeschooling. During the next twelve years, one, two, or all three of my children were being educated at home. Every year, we made a new plan, because I believed the decision to homeschool should be appropriate to that child at that time in his or her life. So, in addition to homeschooling, we explored private school, a co-op, public school and, in 1991, the founding of my own homeschool program. By high school, my children settled into the type of education that worked best for their learning styles. My oldest daughter homeschooled through-out junior high and high school. At an early age, she knew she wanted to be a commercial and film director. Her high school and college years were spent interning with noted directors and established film companies. Her focus, and my faith in her passion, paid off. Today, she is one of the top commercial women directors in the country. My middle child decided that public school was more suited to his needs (with short breaks for homeschooling). He completed his Masters at Harvard and is highly ranked in the military. My youngest son explored all forms of education and ultimately graduated from our homeschool program. Going on to college and becoming a successful visual effects artist, his work is often seen in movies and music videos.

At the time I made the decision to homeschool, it was not an idea whose time had come. I was learning along with my children and experienced a great sense of accomplishment as I discovered that learning could take place in many environments. Looking back, I now know that my children displayed many unique characteristics often associated with homeschoolers: they were independent thinkers, high achievers, highly motivated, multi-talented, and very social. There was also the challenge of explaining to grandparents and friends that my children were getting a good education and they would be productive, successful members of society.

I was one of the early pioneers, and pioneering doesn't come with a roadmap, validation from peers, or immediate evidence of success. Therefore, with support and inspiration from my husband and fellow educators, I co-founded Laurel Springs School, a college prep distance learning program which provides families with the best of homeschooling, combined with all of the benefits of an accredited private school. Now, others can benefit from the knowledge gleaned during those early days, yet shaped to fit the needs of a world that embraces homeschooling, but also requires compliance with regulations and high expectations of performance.

Laurel Springs embraces Rebecca Kochenderfer's approach to learning, as she articulates clear strategies for: discovering your child's unique learning personality, interests, and talents; creating a learning environment; time management; setting goals; and making smart decisions on a daily basis. *Homeschooling and Loving It* provides a roadmap for the homeschooling parent, leading to effective and brilliant end results. Laurel Springs endorses Rebecca Kochenderfer's belief that a college education is a very important goal, and she offers guidelines for students to gain entrance to college. Like Rebecca, Laurel Springs believes children can "live the life they dreamed of now" and prepare for life after high school. We align with Rebecca because the Laurel Springs model of education believes that within every child is a brilliant individual and, given the right tools, support, and environment, children can manifest their dreams and become the highly effective young people they fully deserve to be. In fact, in working with homeschool families for over thirty-five years, I continue to be amazed and awed by the accomplishments of our students and other homeschooled students around the world.

At Laurel Springs, 98% of graduates are accepted to a *college of their choice*. Laurel Springs' graduates are unparalleled in attracting college *scholarships* (over 5.3 million dollars in the last three years). Laurel Springs' graduates gain acceptance into the most *prestigious universities* in the United States, including: Yale, Princeton, Columbia, Wharton School of Business, Harvard, and Stanford. Our students are happy, healthy, participating members of society, excited by learning, and eager to contribute to the world around them. Laurel Springs is a tribute to the bountiful history of homeschooling and the need to personalize education to meet each child's needs.

One of my favorite mentors, Steven Covey, author of *7 Habits of Highly Effective Families,* provides a model of common habits and core values that lead to the creation of an effective family. As homeschooling parents, I believe one of our strongest desires and greatest concerns is ensuring we provide our children with a good education. Covey's work is brought to life in every chapter of *Homeschooling and Loving It*, providing us with goals, tips, and even a customized learning plan to ensure homeschooling families can be highly effective. I hope that Covey's 7 Habits, made real through the work of Rebecca Kochenderfer, will give you the gift of an inspirational journey which supports your students to have a happy, healthy, safe, and inspirational education.

Habit 1: Be Proactive (Become an Agent of Change in Your Family)
Home Schooling families believe a purposeful life is part of the learning process.

Homeschooling allows students to understand they are the masters of their own ships. True motivation comes from within. Achieving one's dreams is the greatest gift a parent can give to a child. At Laurel Springs, we believe actualizing one's dreams is the purpose of education. We encourage students to explore their deepest held hopes and dreams and demonstrate them through core academic subjects, dance, drama, athletics, technology, travel, language, art, and more. *Homeschooling and Loving It* encourages families to become "Agents of Change." It teaches parents how to organize school supplies, understand their child's learning style, and choose an appropriate curriculum that ensures each child will be prepared to graduate, pass high-school level exams, and be accepted to their first-choice college.

Habit 2: Begin with the End in Mind (Develop a Family Mission Statement)
Actualize your mission and vision of reaching your child's education and life goals.

Homeschooling and Loving It encourages families to develop a principle-centered family mission statement. I believe this is the engine that energizes a family to move from their core, out into the world, and demonstrates that a mission-filled life can infuse education with greater meaning. At Laurel Springs, all actions stem from our core values. It's never too early to lay the groundwork for a greater, purpose-filled life.

Habit 3: Put First Things First (Making Family a Priority in a Turbulent World)
Put in place the roles that allow a step-by-step plan to actualize your family mission.

This Third Habit is the very reason for homeschooling, putting you family first. Please don't miss Chapter 6, "8 Keys to Your Life Long Success," which include: Integrity; Knowing that failure leads to success; Speaking with positive purpose and intention; Having a "this is it" attitude; Being present now; Commitment; Ownership; Flexibility; and Balance.

Habit 4: Think Win/Win (Moving from Me to We)
The mastery- based method of education allows for a win/win approach to learning.

This is not about passing or failing. This is not about the teacher winning, or the student losing. This is about both the parent and child benefiting from exploration, where there is no risk of winning or losing. *Homeschooling and Loving It* provides a system of teaching this important methodology and provides a pattern to last a lifetime.

Habit 5: Seek First to Understand, Then to Be Understood (Solving Family Problems Through Empathetic Communication)
Understanding your child's unique learning style provides for academic and personal success.

This habit exemplifies the Learning Style model of education endorsed by both Rebecca and Laurel Springs. By understanding your child's learning personality, interests, and talents, education takes on a new, versatile, and more exciting role. Learning is an inherent and natural part of living and, as we understand and recover our own desire to learn, we provide our students with new pathways for the future.

Habit 6: Synergize (Building Family Unity through Celebrating Differences)
Collaborating and celebrating differences makes it possible for 1+1 to equal 3.

This important habit embraces understanding and valuing differences. Homeschooling builds mutual trust and understanding, the ability to enhance communication, solve problems, resolve conflicts, and bring forth collaborative solutions. The whole becomes greater than the sum of its parts, as we learn how our varied approaches make us better and stronger.

Habit 7: Sharpen the Saw (Renewing the Family Spirit Through Traditions)
Homeschooling allows you to create a balanced approach that supports and nurtures the whole child. Taking time for renewal of the physical, mental, social, and spiritual dimensions.

Learning takes place in many environments. Become life long learners by taking time for field trips and project-based activities. It's not all about homework and schoolwork. It's about living life to the fullest. I've always believed that working with the whole child is the most effective way to realize an educated, healthy person. The balance among physical, mental, social/emotional, and spiritual dimensions provides students with a holistic understanding of themselves and the world around them. And you'll have more fun with your children. Most important, you child will remain "motivated" all year long

To quote Rebecca Kochenderfer: "So relax – you have everything you need. You might as well take your child by the hand and jump in. I promise you this is a journey not to be missed."

Marilyn Mosley Gordanier
Founder/Director, Laurel Springs School
College Prep Distance Learning

INTRODUCTION

I love homeschooling. My husband affectionately calls me a "homeschooling fanatic" and I suppose it's true. I have three children and I have been homeschooling since 1992.

 Not only do I homeschool two of my own children, but I also have the honor of running Homeschool.com, which is the #1 homeschooling site on the Internet. Homeschool.com has over a million readers, so I designed a survey to find out what types of challenges they face from day to day and how they want to improve upon their methods of homeschooling.

This book is structured around addressing the needs and challenges of the hundreds of homeschoolers who answered the Homeschool.com survey. I also included their greatest insights and suggestions about every aspect of homeschooling. So you are getting not only my own experience, but also the advice and experience of thousands of other homeschoolers in the U.S. and abroad.

If you are new to homeschooling, this book can serve as your essential primer to educating kids of all ages, from toddlers to teens. You will learn the basics and then some—what works and what doesn't work as well. I wish I had had this book when I started out. It would have made our homeschooling a lot easier and a lot more fun.

Whether you are a newcomer or a seasoned veteran (I won't say "old-timer"), this book will give you a system to make this *the best year ever* for you and your children. Homeschooling is not just a method of education. It's a lifestyle. We want our children to become lifetime learners not only because it's a wonderfully natural way to be, but also because they will need to be this if they are to keep up in this fast-changing world. The best way to become a lifetime learner is to develop a passion for learning. And the best way to develop that passion is to make learning fun, relevant and fascinating. When you do, you will simply be passing along and sharing in your child's natural joy of learning. This is one of the best ways to create lifelong learners—by making homeschooling fun. It should be educational, yes, but it should be a joy too!

You also create lifelong learners by being one *yourself*. You are a natural teacher. Everyday you are teaching your children by example. This means you need to be curious and interested in life if you want them to be. When you are passionate about learning and they see that you are still learning, they stay curious and inspired. This is actually one of the best parts of homeschooling—while your children are exploring their passions and developing their special talents, you get to explore and develop yours too. Which means, homeschooling is not just something you do for one to four hours a day…it's actually a way of thinking about and approaching life.

I'm a big believer in goal setting. It has worked so well for me throughout my life. Before I regularly set any goals for myself, I often felt lost and confused. I would decide I was going to do something but then I would change gears and move on to something else before I had completed my original intention. This was terrible for my self-esteem. I've learned that one of the best ways to believe in myself is to set do-able goals and to complete those goals. Now, I am a do-er — someone who can be counted on. When I say that I am going to do something, people believe it. Best of all, I believe it too. So I use this same approach with my children. And I will be showing you a failure-proof way to set and achieve goals consistently.

Ever since my children were little I have asked them what they wanted to learn and I built their curriculum around these goals. This has worked so well for us and I think—actually I know—it will work for you too. It's so much easier to stay motivated when you're learning something meaningful. I still remember when my son decided his #1 goal was that he wanted to learn to drive every kind of boat -- so we found a summer camp in our area that would teach him to do just that. He enjoyed that camp for two summers until he reached his goal. He didn't go on to become a sea captain, but that was not the point of goal setting. In addition to his boating lessons, what he learned was to take his dreams seriously, that he can achieve anything he sets out to do, and that his parents support him in fulfilling his dreams. That's pretty powerful stuff.

I encourage you to let go of some of your traditional ways of looking at learning and to try something new. I want you to ask your children what it is that they want to learn and to build your curriculum around that. You're going to be surprised how much more effective and enjoyable this approach is. I think you will see a world of improvement in your children's learning and in their attitudes. Children blossom when they feel valued and heard. I think you'll find that asking your children what they want to learn, and how they like to learn, will open a lot of interesting doors not just for them, but for you also.

I have met a few homeschoolers who talk about how burdened they feel, as if they have forgotten it is a choice, and a fortunate opportunity. It doesn't help anyone if you view homeschooling as a sacrifice, something you have to do. I have been homeschooling for over 16 years and I can personally attest to what a pleasure it can be. This is not to say that every day is rosy and perfect. That's not life. But my children know that I love to homeschool them, that it is a natural extension of who I am and what I enjoy. They see me reading history books, playing with science kits, learning the guitar and writing books and now they want to do these things too. That's role-model parenting at its best.

In truth, this book is about homeschooling yourself as well as your children. I want to help you discover your own dreams, goals and passions in the process. I want to help you rekindle your own love of learning so that you can pass this on to your children. Along the way, you are going to discover so much about yourself and your children. Supporting each other and going for your goals as a team can strengthen your family, will build your children's confidence, and will help shape them into successful and fulfilled young adults.

This book will walk you step-by-step through a system that is guaranteed to help you have your best homeschooling year ever. At the back of the book is your *Custom Home Learning Plan.* At the end of each chapter, I have included an activity for you to do. These activities will help you stay on top of things so that you feel one step ahead of the game all year long. If you diligently read each chapter, then complete the activity, by the end of this book you are going to have in your hands a fun, customized learning plan for each of your children--one that takes into account each child's learning style, interests and goals. It will also take into account your schedule, interests and teaching style. You will be amazed at how much you accomplish! For example:

- **Your school supplies will be organized**
- **You will know your child's learning style and curriculum for the year**
- **You will have worked with your child to set semester and longer term goals**
- **You will have a more efficient day-to-day schedule that's balanced with your own life**
- **You will develop a system of teaching that works best for you and your child**
- **Your child will be prepared to graduate high-school level exams and get into their first-choice college**
- **You will have more fun with your children, so you and your "students" will stay motivated all year long**

I've also filled each chapter with online resources that will support you from Day 1 right through graduation. So relax—you have everything you need. You might as well take your child by the hand and jump in.

Please write to me at Editor@Homeschool.com and tell me what you discover about your children's dreams and about your own dreams. I would love to hear your stories.

Warmly wishing you all the best with your homeschooling!

Rebecca Kochenderfer

Cofounder and Editor in Chief
Homeschool.com
2008

FOR NEWCOMERS...

Frequently Asked Questions About Homeschooling

♥ Q: What is homeschooling?

A: Homeschooling is the most flexible and diverse educational option available today. The variety of homeschooling styles reflects the diversity of the people who choose this method. Some families organize their homeschool to be the same as a traditional school, with the children studying the same subjects the same way as public school students. Some families use the opposite approach and "un-school" their children -- a far less structured approach where the children's schedule is determined by their interests and readiness. Most homeschoolers, however, use an eclectic approach that is partly structured and partly free flowing. This method allows parents to pick and choose the classes and materials that meet their children's needs. These may be college or co-op classes, online classes, charter schools, independent study programs, apprenticeships, volunteering, or a host of other options. Homeschooling is as unique as you are.

♥ Q: What types of families homeschool their children?

A: Although homeschoolers are often stereotyped as hippies or religious fanatics, most homeschoolers are just "normal" parents who have decided to take charge of their children's education. Homeschoolers are everywhere and come from all walks of life. They live in cities, in the suburbs, and in the country. They are doctors, janitors and public school teachers. Some homeschoolers have strong religious beliefs and some are nonbelievers. Homeschoolers are just like you.

♥ Q: Is homeschooling legal?

A: Homeschooling is legal in all fifty states and throughout Canada. Homeschooling is also becoming increasingly popular in Australia, New Zealand, England, and Japan. However, every state and province has its own laws regarding homeschooling and some are more "friendly" than others. Some homeschooling laws merely require you to let your local school district know that you will be homeschooling your children. Some laws require you to fill out paperwork as if you were a private school. If you are considering homeschooling, you will need to get information on the laws in your area. State or local homeschool groups are often the best source for this information. A member of a support group in your state can advise you on how to register as a homeschooler.

♥ Q: How much does homeschooling cost?

A: Depending on the choices you make, homeschooling can cost either a little or a lot. Generally, you can assume that homeschooling costs more than a public school education but less than a private school. If you had to, you could homeschool for free using public resources like libraries, PBS shows, museums, the Internet, and hand-me-down educational supplies. In general, homeschooling costs more if you use a boxed curriculum or sign up with a curriculum provider. Homeschooling costs are higher for teenagers than for elementary school students, and fees are normally charged on a per class basis. Since many homeschool teens also take college classes, you will have to factor that into your educational budget. You will also want to budget additional funding for extracurricular activities such as soccer, gymnastics, martial arts, piano lessons, and the like. Since homeschooled children have more time, they tend to participate in more of these activities. The bottom line is: (1) You have complete control over how much homeschooling will cost and (2) you can give your child a quality education no matter how much or how little money you have.

♥ Q: What are the advantages of homeschooling?

A: For many homeschoolers, one of the greatest benefits of homeschooling is the strengthening of family bonds. Homeschooling families spend a lot of time learning and playing together and this naturally creates close ties between brothers and sisters and between children and parents. Homeschoolers also have a great deal of flexibility in how and what they learn, allowing them to learn about the "real world" by being part of it. These advantages allow homeschooled children to receive a superior education that is attuned specifically to their own needs, learning style, personality and interests.

♥ Q: What are the disadvantages of homeschooling?

A: According to homeschoolers' feedback on Homeschool.com, the biggest disadvantage facing the homeschooling family is loss of income. Someone must be home, at least part-time, to facilitate the children's learning. At a time when it can often be difficult to get by on two incomes, it can be a real challenge to get by on just one. Some of the other difficulties facing homeschooling parents include lack of confidence in their own and their children's abilities, public and/or family criticism, and adjusting career goals and work schedules to accommodate the needs of the family. One last challenge humorously cited by homeschoolers is that of housekeeping. When you use your home full-time for homeschooling (and in some cases even for work), things can get a bit messy. But don't worry, those books piled high on the coffee table, the science experiment on the table and the art projects in the patio, are all signs that your child is learning.

♥ Q: How are homeschooled students doing socially?

A: It used to be that if you announced you were going to homeschool your children people would ask you, "How will your children learn anything?" Now that fears have been put to rest regarding homeschoolers' academic achievement, the most commonly asked question is, "But what about socialization?" The assumption is that children will not learn to get along with others and will not develop good social skills unless they go to school. However, several studies have been conducted over the years that show that homeschooled children are more self-confident and less peer dependent than traditionally schooled students. Many people believe that homeschoolers spend all their time around the kitchen table, but that simply is not the case. Since homeschooled students do not spend six hours a day in a classroom sitting behind a desk, they have more time to participate in activities outside the home, such as in music, sports, and Scouts. Also, whereas school children rarely have the opportunity to interact with the children who are not the same age, homeschooled children interact with and learn from people of all ages, genders and interests.

♥ Q: Will my children be able to get into college if they are homeschooled?

A: Homeschoolers are accepted and recruited by some of the top universities in the country because of their maturity, independent thinking skills, creativity and strong academic preparation. In general, homeschoolers perform above average on the ACT. Success on the ACT reveals that the courses taken by high school students to prepare for college have been effective. Homeschoolers also placed highest on the SAT college entrance exams in the year 2000. In addition to academic success, homeschoolers have had athletic success in college. Coaches are recruiting homeschooled athletes, and in 2001 the National Collegiate Athletic Association (NCAA) declared about 100 homeschooled students eligible for athletics as freshmen at major universities, up from 85 the year before. An article in Time magazine on September 11, 2000, reported that 26 percent of 35 homeschooled applicants had been accepted into Stanford University's 2000-2001 freshman class. This is nearly double the rate of overall acceptances.

♥ Q: Will my children be able to succeed in the "real world" if they do not go to school?

A: Those exploring homeschooling for the first time sometimes worry that their child will not be able to function in the "real world" if they don't attend school and have the same social experiences as schooled children. But what do schools *really* do? They separate kids by age and ability and limit their interactions to short recess periods. School children are forced to socialize with children only their own age and are trapped in a room six to seven hours a day and allowed to view the outside world only through a textbook. Where in the real world are adults forced to socialize with only people their own age? Competition, bullying, consumerism, and cruel teasing are often the social values children learn at school. Homeschooled children are more likely to base their decisions on values they learned from their parents instead of feeling compelled to go along with the crowd and accept the behavior of what other children are displaying as the "norm." Because homeschoolers spend so much time out in the real world, they are able to communicate well and get along with both adults and children. They even get along with their siblings, and it is common for homeschooling families to receive positive comments about their children's strong, warm sibling relationships.

♥ Q: Can I homeschool if I'm overseas?

A: Homeschooling is growing in popularity around the world, particularly in Australia, New Zealand, South Africa, the United Kingdom, and Japan. Still, homeschooling originated in the United States, and because of that there are more homeschooling resources and opportunities available in America than anywhere else. If you are an American living overseas, you can use an American independent study program to help you while you are away. If you plan on living overseas for an extended period of time and your child is in high school, you may want to consider participating in the international baccalaureate program, which gives your child an international diploma that she or he can use for admittance to some of the finest universities in the world.

CHAPTER ONE

QUICK-START HOMESCHOOLING PLAN

- ♥ **Get Ready...Get Set!**
- ♥ **Face Your Challenges**
- ♥ **Learn Your State's Requirements**
- ♥ **Go!**

Homeschooling means many things to many people. There are as many ways to learn as there are to teach. Different families homeschool their children for different reasons. Regardless of *why* we homeschool, what really matters is that our children learn effectively, and that it's fun and rewarding for both parents and kids.

Learning is a lifelong endeavor. I have gotten so much out of my 16 years of homeschooling--maybe even more than my children have! I've loved every year. And every year has been different as my three children have reached different ages, followed their unique interests, and excelled in ways that just absolutely amaze me.

♥ Note to Newcomers

For those of you who are just starting out, homeschooling can be scary at first, but you're never going it alone. There are 3 million homeschoolers in the United States alone. We're all over the country and there is also an entire online community you can tap into. Chances are, there will be other homeschoolers in your community, maybe even in your neighborhood. Many homeschooling families go on project outings together, exchange learning materials, and share secrets of what's worked for them over the years. You can simply find them by posting online. And…now you have *this* book, which will walk you through every step with your child for the first year and beyond.

♥ Could I Be a Great Homeschooler?

Anyone who has ever considered homeschooling as an option, but hasn't made the leap, has asked themselves the burning question: "Do I have what it takes?" And when people ask themselves this, they're usually wondering, "Am I smart enough? Will I have enough time in my schedule? Could I really provide them a great education? "

Here's the simple answer to all three questions…YES! No matter who you are, where you live or what your circumstances are, you will be able to effectively homeschool your child or children at any age and prepare them for college, even if you yourself don't have that same level of formal education. You just need to have the desire and know your local high school diploma requirements. The rest is a matter of fostering a love of learning in your children. And the good news is that they probably already do love to learn. If you've watched your toddler you already know that kids have a curiosity about life, about people, and about how things work, including themselves. And they are constantly exploring. At any age, this natural desire to understand continues. Your job is simply to guide them and provide the resources and environment they need to continue this lifelong pursuit of knowledge. Here's how one homeschooler describes it:

> *"Our curriculum is LIFE! Whatever we encounter during our day, I take the opportunity to talk to the girls about it. My six-year-old knows a ton about astronomy, just by sitting on the front porch at night and discussing the stars. She also knows a great deal about the weather, as her father is a storm spotter. She's learned a lot about us and world geography because we watch the weather maps and discuss storm formation. Filling our bookshelves with high-quality books about a wide variety of subjects has created an academic smorgasbord for the girls, and they are eating it up!"*

There is no absolute right or wrong way to educate. One thing every experienced homeschooler will tell you is:

***You* are the homeschooling expert when it comes to your child.**

Certainly it benefits you to consider all advice and resources that come your way. Just remember, your child and life circumstances are unique and what works well for another family might not be right for your family. One of homeschooling's numerous benefits is that as the expert, *you* can pick and choose what's best for your child. You will be amazed by how much you both learn about each other, what works, and what doesn't work in the process. As one homeschooler observed, *"No matter how messed up your first year seems, it's the best growing experience you and your children will ever have."*

That is so true! I have tried a variety of different teaching methods and I have researched every option there is out there to find the best of the best for my own children's particular learning styles and goals. Together we've honed their curricula each year. I developed my own style of teaching, learned (the hard way sometimes) how to organize learning materials and supplies (as well as my time), and learned to coordinate the daily, monthly and yearly goals of each child and worked them all around my own chores and personal time. Then of course there was budgeting for all this, while still making it creative enough to keep us all motivated and having fun.

Phew! Luckily, it's easier than it sounds! More importantly, it is SO richly rewarding. The time you get to spend with your children is priceless. I so enjoy watching my children as they explore the world. Homeschooling is such a creative endeavor; you will ultimately find your own ways of teaching and balancing your schedule with your children's goals.

♥ Benefits of Homeschooling

All children have a natural desire to understand nature, people and their own abilities…so why do we even need homeschooling? Well, it gives them structure and motivation. Even when they're not studying, they stay engaged in life. They follow their interests, and develop their gifts. They have the time and flexibility to develop their skills in whatever area they choose. They have the self-confidence of someone who has been allowed to determine their own goals, then reach them one after the other. They're self-motivated too. They're not just completing tasks set before them and waiting on a grade. Instead, they initiate and follow-through on their own projects. This means that they've developed their minds to conceptualize, focus, and then achieve whatever they want. This makes them truly prepared to deal well with life after school and all the new experiences it will bring to them. They will be able to stay on their toes and be adaptive and resourceful in an ever-changing world culture and economy. They've learned how to be lifelong learners and thinkers. Now they know they are capable of accomplishing great things -- essentially, anything they set their mind to.

Obviously, there's a whole lot that could be said on the benefits of homeschooling. Just in case I'm preaching to the choir here, let's move on to cover what a lot of you seasoned homeschoolers expressed you need help with, some of the more persistent challenges you have, ways you now want to improve your results.

♥ Common Challenges Facing Homeschoolers

In a recent Homeschool.com survey I asked homeschoolers:

1. *What is the #1 improvement you would like to make to your homeschooling?*

2. *What is the biggest obstacle or challenge you face in achieving that?*

I anticipated the responses to the survey would most likely be about the challenges faced trying to teach difficult subjects like algebra or science. Instead, over three hundred people said that the #1 IMPROVEMENT they wanted to make would be to…survey says…!

#1—Be better organized   #2—Have more money   #3—Have more fun

And the #1 CHALLENGE or OBSTACLE homeschoolers face in making those improvements…TIME!

I researched and gathered the best information on these specific areas from the experts—educators and other experienced homeschoolers -- as well as from my own experience and I put together these 7 Proven Steps for Successful Homeschooling:

7 Proven Steps for Successful Homeschooling

STEP 1:   Set goals based on your child's interests.

STEP 2:   Discover your child's learning style.

STEP 3:   Assess your curriculum yearly. Decide on your semester and daily schedule and adapt your teaching style to match your child's learning style.

STEP 4:   Budget for products, tutors and materials to support these goals.

STEP 5:   Organize your time to manage your life and peace of mind.

STEP 6:   Prepare for high school graduation and college.

STEP 7:   Create a Custom Home Learning Plan for each of your children.

♥ Grade Expectations

If you're already a homeschooler, you probably have worried at one point or another, "Is my child keeping up with kids of his or her age group?"

Well, I really want to comfort you about this. There really are no specific expectations for each grade. At least no one agrees on these expectations.

**Isn't it interesting...
Education requirements differ from state to state, but
as long as you expect the best from your child,
you are likely to exceed any government standards.**

Quite frankly, what the state requires of children is far less than what they are capable of achieving. If you and your child are like most homeschooling families, your child will end up surpassing state requirements. The requirement are often very different from what parents come to know their children can achieve, and different still from the goals children have for themselves.

"I am instilling a love of learning. My family always talks about college, and we've visited our alumni schools. The kids know that they are expected to go to college. Right now, we focus on learning and all the ways one can do this for a lifetime. High school is merely a place to get free classes, and college is a place to earn a degree. The luckiest students, though, learn in spite of requirements from institutions."

There are so many types of primary school education programs and different requirements from state to state, that there is no one right answer to the question, "What does my child need to know by the end of our homeschool year?" Schools all have different expectations for what they think should be accomplished by the end of each grade. For example, Waldorf schools like to give their students time to mature and do not teach reading until the second grade. However, there are some private schools that expect preschoolers to already be reading, and Classical homeschoolers do things differently than Charlotte Mason homeschoolers.

Actually, grade-level expectations are pretty random. And to be honest, isn't our goal to do *better than* the public schools? Not just meet their standards? So I want to encourage you not to worry about standardized grade-level expectations and instead to set goals with your children each year that will give them an excellent education that is based on developing their special passions and talents. This is the real beauty of homeschooling and an advantage for you—there is no rigid set of rules about *what, when* or *how* they should learn. In this book you'll find guidelines for a *what, when* and *how* approach that has worked well for hundreds of homeschoolers. But remember, *you* are the expert regarding your own children.

If you have been homeschooling for awhile you probably already know what the homeschooling laws are for your area. But in case you are new to homeschooling, I want to make sure you feel assured that you're on top of any legal issues so that you can really focus on the more important task at hand—being a great parent and teacher. Later chapters will even cover testing and portfolio requirements so that you can feel confident that you are preparing your kids all along the way to meet and exceed college acceptance guidelines too.

♥ How Do I Make Sure My Child Stays At or Above Grade Level?

Google It

Your initial research can be done on the Internet. You can easily find out everything you need to know about your state's education guidelines by going to "Google" or "Yahoo" or any of the other search engines. **Enter the name of your state and then the words "grade-level expectations."**

This will bring up links to sites that will list the laws in your state, and specific requirements for math, science, and reading. These will give you guidelines to meet if you are required to take standardized tests each year. These tests simply compare your student with other students in the state and tell you generally what percentile your child is in within the average scoring for their age group.

Ask Other Homeschoolers in Your Area

The best way to find out about the homeschooling laws in your area is to contact a homeschooling group in your local town. They are the real experts. Ask them what you need to do. They will probably know every nuance of the system and can communicate it more directly than all the state's documents online.

Some states require annual testing. Some require you to submit a portfolio each semester or year. Some states allow you to join a charter school or "umbrella school." Find out what documentation you will need to submit and when you have to submit it.

Be sure to ask more than one person, because there are lots of right ways to follow homeschooling laws.

Read Up on the Subject

There are a few great resources I recommend for determining your own standards for learning. My family really likes the *What Every 1ˢᵗ Grader Should Know* series by E.D. Hirsh. This series includes books for grades K through 6. My family has worn our copies to tatters. You may also get a lot out of a book called *The Well-Trained Mind* by Susan Wise Bauer. Her method of classical homeschooling is very popular with homeschoolers. Rebecca Rupp has a good book called *Home Learning Year by Year*. These will enable you to gauge a long-term trajectory of where you want your kids to be along the way, with a focus on their intellectual development. Chances are your children will soon exceed your state's grade expectations anyway.

Since you are both parent *and* teacher, I've set up an activity for you at the end of each chapter. Consider these writing sessions like Parent/Teacher conferences. It's important to take the time for yourself so that you can:

- ❤ Find out how you can better serve your child's needs
- ❤ Keep your child's schedule and supplies organized all year
- ❤ Be time-efficient so that you and your children can accomplish your year and semester goals

This first assignment is mostly for you. You might also choose to share the local education laws with your children. After doing your research, it's a good idea to write down or print out your state's requirements and keep them in a workbook or another special place. Maybe you want to post them on the wall somewhere or keep them close to your calendar. Make sure to record any specific due dates on the master calendar that we will put together in a later chapter.

ACTIVITY

Our State's Requirements

Object of the Game
Fulfill legal requirements so that you can focus on your child's development.

Step 1 – Research your state's requirements

Research your state's grade-level expectations for each of your children. Do your own Internet search. Visit your local library and ask for the reference book on educational standards in your state. Go to a bookstore or to Amazon.com and take a look at the books I mentioned. Do a Google search with the name of your state and the words "grade-level expectations" in quotation marks.

Step 2 – Write them down

Write down or print out your state's educational requirements for each of your children. What are the homeschooling laws for your area? Are you required to take tests or submit learning records or forms? Are there state testing dates and locations?

Be sure to write down any testing dates on your semester calendar too. This can be your "at a glance" reference point in case you forget them and want to make sure you're keeping your children's learning on schedule for their age. Find out where state tests are being conducted.. Your child may be able to go to a local school on those dates to take the tests with other children.

Step 3 – Keep a copy on hand for easy reference when you're developing your semester goals

In a later chapter, you and your child will be coming up with some personal goals as well as semester goals. Refer to your state's requirements and testing dates in case there are specific goals they need to reach by certain dates. You will want to include them in their Custom Home Learning Plan when you are developing their curriculum for that semester.

CHAPTER TWO

THE BEST TEACHING STYLE

- ♥ **Define the Word "Success"**
- ♥ **Be a Lighthouse**
- ♥ **Have Fun**
- ♥ **Create a Mission Statement**

As a teacher, you teach through the curriculum. As a parent, you teach by example. As a homeschooler, character and values automatically become part of what you're teaching, whether you intend them to or not. So the best teaching style is, of course, by example.

Be a lighthouse, not a flashlight. You have a choice here. You can run around on the beach with a flashlight trying to please everyone. Or you can be a lighthouse. Shine your own solid, powerful light, and the ships will come to you.

Sometimes as homeschoolers, we run around trying to keep up with a regimented schedule of courses, and all the while our actions are speaking louder than our words. So I say, let's be a lighthouse to our children with our homeschooling this coming year.

Let's not give in to fear and conform to public school standards at home just because we're afraid our kids might miss something. Take a chance this semester and work with your child's interests and passions. You can always adjust along the way if you feel something isn't working or if you feel you're missing something important. What you show your children through who you are and what you do is just as important as any subject. Don't let the curriculum drive *you*. You drive *it*. Use it as your tool, not as your taskmaster. The curriculum is your guide, but *you* are the beacon.

♥ Teach By Example

So what's the best teaching style? Teaching by example. When you're homeschooling your children this semester, remember that you are focusing not *only* on skills, but on character and integrity. Skills are "what you know." Character is "who you are." The word integrity comes from the algebra word "integer" which means "whole". Integrity is being a whole, complete person. Some people are like a circle, divided in half. They act one way in one situation and another way in a different situation. For example, they're nice to a person they see as important, yet they treat their waitress like dirt. Their character then is inconsistent so they are out of integrity.

Homeschooler's Checklist

Do you have?

- ☐ **Character and Values?**
- ☐ **Your Own Personal Goals?**
- ☐ **A Love of Learning?**
- ☐ **Fun?**
- ☐ **A Desire to See Your Child Thrive?**

Then you'll be a great homeschooler!

When it comes to integrity and character, children learn through role-modeling. There's a saying, "What you do speaks so loudly I can't hear a word you say." In other words, we can't tell them how important it is to read, but never pick up a book ourselves. We can't tell them to be honest, and then when someone calls whisper, "Tell them I'm not home." We can't tell them that we want them to dream big, but then put off our own dreams. This is why the chapter assignments throughout this book are as much about you as they are about your child. Doing the activities throughout the book before you guide your children in their own "learning games," will help you lead by example.

♥ How Do You Define "Success"?

What do you really want for your children? How do you define success? It's important that we start with the big picture here. Then we will work our way back down to daily scheduling and subject goals. If we want our children to be successful, we have to know exactly what successful is. Success means different things to different people. What I want for my kids may not be exactly what you want for yours. Yet, we can still take a big picture approach to teaching. Start with what you're aiming to accomplish.

I've given this a lot of thought and here's what I've come up with. This is what I want for my children:

1) I want my children to have a strong foundation in the basics, including reading, writing, math, history, and science.
2) I want my children to be curious life-long learners who are open to learning new things and who know how to research and learn about anything they are interested in.
3) I want them to have the courage to go after their dreams and I want them to know how to use goal setting to achieve those dreams.
4) I want to bring out my children's special gifts and show them how to use these gifts to their fullest. My children are still young and the proof is in the pudding, but I'll feel like I've succeeded as a parent and that my children are a success if . . .
   - They wake up in the morning eager to start the day.
   - They know that they can go to Harvard, if they want to.
   - They have good business skills and feel confident in their ability to earn any amount of money they want to earn.
   - They grow up to feel good about their lives and what they're creating.

I guess my definition of "success" then, is that they are enjoying life and have the expectation that more good things are just around the corner, and that they believe anything is possible.

Coming up, I'm going to ask you to answer the questions: "What is your definition of success?" and "What do you really want for your children?" But before we do that, let's talk about a very integral part of your children's education—helping them find and fulfill their life purpose.

♥ Let Them Pursue Their Passions and Purpose

This may sound like a lofty goal. You're just trying to figure out if you have what it takes to teach biology, right? And here I am talking about having a greater sense of purpose behind their learning. Well, don't feel overwhelmed...

Starting with a sense of purpose, fun, and appreciation will make everything else fall into place. With this foundation, teaching and learning becomes a whole lot easier.

And don't worry; very few people can actually articulate what their "purpose" is. It's probably not just one thing anyway. But if you just allow your children to follow their interests and what they're passionate about, they may soon feel at least that life has more meaning and purpose. And, they will be more motivated than you've ever seen them.

Marilyn Mosley has built Laurel Springs School on the idea that the purpose of homeschooling is for a child to fulfill his or her purpose in life, and that everyone has a purpose, including us parents. She has had amazing success with this approach to teaching, many talented kids who were allowed to pursue their interests, graduated and became very successful in their fields. I interviewed Marilyn a couple of years ago as part of Homeschool.com's Summer Homeschooling Teleconference. Here is a short excerpt from that interview. As you read, think about how you can apply Marilyn's advice in teaching your own children.

Marilyn Mosley: *Children, adults, we all have a purpose for being here, a reason for being on the earth, a life purpose. That can so easily be excluded from our view by just a day-to-day busy-ness of the world, and the kinds of focuses that are becoming prevalent. It's so important to let children know that they are important and they have a reason for being here... Allow children to feel that they are important, that they are here for more than just acquiring goods and services or even just information. They are here to do work that is important and that can help others...Every single child has ideas about what he or she wants to be when they grow up. They might tell you they want to be an astronaut or a movie director or a fireman. These dreams are sort of the seeds to their life purpose.*

Usually, beneath the surface is a desire to do good work and be helpful, to make a difference in the world. So, it's really important to acknowledge those early dreams. Time is one of the most precious commodities we have with our children; it's something that most children going to school don't have, and they don't have the time to think clearly. Homeschooling gives them the time to develop their self-esteem, and to also develop their talents and gifts in a loving and protected environment.

20

One of the most important tools, and I think it's something that is true for life in general, is what I call the power of appreciation. When a child feels appreciated, when an adult feels appreciated, when any of us feels appreciated, we feel free to become our best self. First is the power of appreciation, the second is to not thwart a child's idea. I remember when my daughter first told me she was going to be a movie director, I could have said to her, "That's completely impossible, how are you going to do that?" Well, she knew by the age of fourteen that she was going to be a director and by the time she was eighteen she was already a successful director out in the world. She could never have done this if we hadn't homeschooled and if she hadn't felt that her dream was being supported.

The other thing that is very important is to give children time to daydream. One thing that has happened in the world is that children are very busy. Their time is being scheduled hour by hour. When children are homeschooled, we can give them time to daydream, time to play -- which is so important for developing their dream.

Another important key is to have a lack of peer pressure. There was a study done by Antioch College that showed homeschooled children tend to miss the second level of development in high school which is the need for peer acceptance. They went from first homeschooling to having a reason, a mission or a purpose. And they didn't need their peers to acknowledge and approve of what they doing.

If we wait to dream, what we're doing is we're establishing a habit. It says that there is another time, a better time, to really become ourselves. When we do that we develop the ability to put off becoming our true selves. We don't do it when we're a child; then, when we're a teenager we're busy being a teenager, and when we're an adult we're often busy earning a living. That ability to develop a life purpose or have a dream starts to fade.

When children develop this muscle from the very beginning, they develop the faith and the confidence in themselves that lets them know that they are capable of having a dream and then pursuing that dream. Children who journal, for example, who have a daily diary in which they jot down their ideas and are allowed to come up with their own inventions (if they're an inventive person), or their own creations (if they're a creative person), tend to be more in touch with their own dreams and their own life purposes.

I want to highlight a couple of Marilyn's points here because they're just so inspiring:

- ♥ Let children know that they are important, and that they have a reason and purpose for being.
- ♥ Appreciate their uniqueness.
- ♥ Acknowledge their dreams. Don't thwart any of their goals.
- ♥ Give them time to daydream and develop their ideas.

If we learned to "put off becoming our true selves," when we were young, then we need to be especially careful that we don't allow ourselves to pass along that same lesson to our children.

If you find one day that you are having a bad day, pause for a minute and do whatever you need to do to "find your smile." There's no need for you to force things, and forcing doesn't work anyway. Instead, take a break and get back into good shape so that you and your children can be your best.

♥ Catch Them Being Good

I want to talk for a minute about the importance of affirming the positive. This has everything to do with what Marilyn Mosley said about "the power of appreciation." We as parents use the word "no" so often with our children. And we spend an awful lot of time criticizing our children or focusing on what they *haven't* done yet. I'm guilty of this too. This can't be good for our children's spirits. There has to be a better way to correct and redirect them, without breaking their spirit.

> **Guilt is a detrimental, and ultimately ineffective, motivator.**
> **While appreciation and positive reinforcement is**
> **powerful motivation that can last a lifetime.**

If you recognize that criticism is as an issue between you and your children, make it a main priority this year to "catch them being good." Include "acknowledging the positive" in your family's mission statement. "Stop the clock" when you notice anything negative coming out of your mouth. Be aware of the effect your words and tone have on your children. Instead of noticing when the bed is *un*made, compliment them when the bed *is* made. Instead of constantly nagging them about the projects they *haven't* finished, put stars on the refrigerator for every little thing that they *do* complete. It may mean developing some new ways of speaking to them, because the criticizing habit is so ingrained. It's what our society does. But as homeschoolers, we have the chance to set the bar a lot higher. Even if it takes concentrated effort on your part, and you slip sometimes, write it down as one of your own assignments. You don't want your children to internalize your critical, unappreciative voice for the rest of their lives.

I include myself in this. Let's make a commitment right now that 80% of what we say to our children is going to be positive. And if we have to correct our children, let's make sure we do it gently and in a way that they can learn from whatever they did wrong.

The definition of self-esteem is "holding yourself in high regard, as a valuable entity." Let's remember to tell our kids that there's nobody like them in the whole wide world. They are special and valued just the way they are.

Encourage children to do what they love to do. Here too is another opportunity to be good examples for our kids. Let's show them that spending time with them and homeschooling them is a joy and a privilege…not a sacrifice. It doesn't mean that you have to be perfect or that homeschooling is going to fun 100% of the time every single day, but…

♥ Focus on Fun

When I was first homeschooling, I used a standardized curriculum and a regimented schedule. This approach may work well for some homeschoolers, but it wasn't for us. My children and I sat around the kitchen table and labored through subjects in the same way they would have if they were at school until I finally realized, I was just as bored as they were! And it was a whole lot more difficult than it needed to be.

There is no one right way to do homeschooling. There's also really no "wrong" way. But, there is a way to do it that is a whole lot harder for you and your child. And you'll know when that's happening because learning and teaching won't be fun. So by "wrong" I just mean, in a way that isn't fun.

Isn't it interesting…
…Learning and assimilating information happens best
when the student is having FUN!

How do you make learning fun? That depends. What sparks your child's curiosity? What makes her eyes light up in wonder? What does she consider fun? Do all these things and more. These activities will lead your child to the act of discovery, the source of successful educational experiences. Beginners sometimes worry that such activities won't lead to learning. However, homeschooling families find curiosity creates interest; interest increases attention to the task at hand; attention gives rise to learning. As you play with and explore your child's interests you'll get better at recognizing the educational value of the activities and learn to incorporate the concepts and information you wish to add.

Visit the library (often!), get out and explore what happens in your community all day and include your child in household activities like gardening, pet care, home repairs and more. Plan interesting field trips. Have fun and enjoy the opportunity to observe and get to know your child better. But don't buy too many materials yet!

Here's a thought...

- ❤ Relax. If you act as if learning is a difficult endeavor, your child will start believing it is. Remember, you're the expert! You're also their role model.

- ❤ Relax again. Observe your child to see and understand what's fun for her.

- ❤ And now take a deep breath and relax. What you do isn't as important as the spirit in which you do it.

Here are a few great ideas to make sure fun is a part of your child's homeschooling experience...

Have a little 'NOT back to school' celebration! In my house it seems like I am always competing with the schools because my oldest daughter attends school and that option is in our life every day. I have to constantly show my son and my youngest daughter that homeschooling is just as good as (and really lots more fun than) school.

Tomorrow we are celebrating the "first day of school." My oldest will be going to her first day of high school. And my son and youngest daughter are getting together with  another homeschooling family to buy school supplies and go out to lunch. When the neighborhood kids call my kids up, talking about how exciting their first day was, I want my kids to have something exciting to say too. I never had to play this game before, but it seems to be important now. This weekend the whole family is going to the mall to have back-to-school photos taken.

Do you want to do something special? Have you asked your kids if they'd like to start their homeschooling with a fun family outing? Maybe do something with another homeschooling family? They can even tell the kids who are complaining about going back to school that they are having a "NOT back to school" party.

For your first couple of weeks of homeschooling, really focus on the fun. Maybe take the kids out to breakfast and fill out the Custom Home Learning Plan with each of them. Perhaps do some research to find out where you can go in the area for some fun field trips. Maybe even explore where the kids can go for fun volunteering activities. I'm going to work with my children to create some sort of goals chart or mural for their bedroom wall so that they can see their goals every day and keep track of how well they are doing on them.

Beginnings and endings are so important, so remember to keep it light and fun in the beginning and then ramp up slowly. Most important, remember to celebrate every time you and your child achieve a goal. Go to dinner, make a cake or call grandma. Do something to pat them on the back. And save a pat for you too. Enjoy a treat, quiet time alone with a novel, or a luxury bath.

SUGGESTION BOX

What Other Homeschoolers Say About Teaching…

"If I could change the way I did anything when I first began to homeschool 13 years ago, I would relax and laugh more. Read aloud, recite poetry, memorize more scripture and poetry, and lots more music for listening. I would hold them more and talk to them about their dreams and their ideas."

"I've approached our homeschool with the mindset that learning should take place every day of our lives. So my husband and I have decided to school year round, at least three days a week. Consequently, we have a much more relaxed, less-pressured mentality about it. And, we end up getting a lot more done."

Family On a Mission
(for parents and kids)

Object of the Game
Share what's important to you about homeschooling so that you can grow together as a team.

Step 1 - Jot down your thoughts and share answers with your children.

You and your children will be writing down your goals in the next few chapters and you may find that your children exceed your expectations. But what you want for your children may not be what they want for themselves. Here is your chance to communicate the expectations you have for homeschooling in general, and become more aware of what values and goals you share in common. Sometimes we even have expectations that we're unaware we have, that we never communicate to the kids. Or perhaps you and your spouse have different expectations—this is the time to formulate what you both want your children to get out of homeschooling.

Do you have personal expectations for your children? What are *your* grade-level expectations for your children this year? Do you have an overview of what you want your children to know before they graduate high school? What do you hope they accomplish in life? What values would you like to see them demonstrating? Write down any thoughts you have about this here.

_____
_____
_____
_____
_____

Step 2 – Answer the following questions and complete these statements:

♥ *What is important to you about homeschooling?*

_____

♥ *What do you hope to achieve by homeschooling your children?*

_____

♥ *I will consider our homeschooling and my parenting to be a success if my children grow up to…*

_____

♥ *Our major goal in our homeschooling is to teach our children…*

_____

Ask these questions of everyone. Have everyone call out words and ideas that are important to them. Different people may repeat the same qualities, like "honesty," "hard work," "discipline," "fun," "freedom." These will be your shared values. You can post this list in your family work/play space. It will help you keep your eye on the ball as a parent to make sure that you are always parenting and homeschooling according to your values and priorities.

Step 3 – From the list, create a family Mission Statement together

The answers to the questions in Step 1 and 2 will help you get a clear image of your family's overall values, your purpose for homeschooling, and your personal definition of success.

Our family created a family mission statement a couple of years ago and this is how we did it. I asked the whole family to come to the table just for 10 to15 minutes. I handed out index cards and asked them to write down the things we do as a family that they like the most, and the things that they would like us to do – the things they think are important and fun. After the meeting, I gathered the cards and wrote a list of all the suggestions. Then, the next week, I asked everyone to get together again for 10-15 minutes to vote for the five or so activities on the list that were their favorites. (We did this as a secret ballot, to keep the suspense.) Then, a couple of days later I showed them the results. We discovered that for our family, our favorite activities are learning new things, traveling and learning languages, camping, and family game night. We then wrote up a couple of sentences for each in pretty calligraphy and put it in a frame. Most importantly, we make sure we take time for these activities. Tuesday night is family game night and we seldom miss it. (We didn't know the kids enjoyed this so much. Even the teenagers!) And we make sure we take a family camping trip every summer. Finding out what's important to our family has also made us notice what's important to other families. We know one family that is totally into athletics, another into music, and another for whom art is the priority. What is important to your family? What are your favorite activities? Ask your kids. You may be surprised.

CHAPTER THREE

GO FOR THE GOALS

♥ **Imagine All You Want to Do in Life**
♥ **Set Semester Goals**
♥ **Go for It!**

When my son was about ten, I asked him this question: "What do you want to learn about this semester?" He said, "I want to learn how to drive every kind of boat." You could have knocked me over with a feather. I had not expected that as an answer. I had no idea he was interested in boats. And, at that point, I also had no idea how a ten-year-old could learn to "drive boats."

I took my son's boat-driving goal very seriously. I told him, "Okay, I don't know how we're going to accomplish this, but we'll figure out how." There was no Internet in those days, so I began asking everyone I knew, "Do you know where a ten-year-old can go to learn about boats?" A lot of people looked at me like I was crazy. Finally, a friend told me that there was a kids' boating camp held every summer, put on by our local university. The camp was five days long. One day they did canoes, the next kayaks, the next day sailboats, then windsailing, and finally motorboats. Can you believe that? It was if the class had been designed just to help my child achieve his goal.

I learned a valuable lesson that day:

> **No matter how crazy or impossible a child's goal seems,**
> **take the dream seriously and you'll find a way to achieve it.**

♥ Why Goals Are Important

Where do you find positive motivation from day to day? Here is a quotation from an interview I did with Wally "Famous Amos." Yes, the guy who makes the cookies. He's also a world-renowned author, inspirational speaker and winner of several awards for promoting literacy and education:

> *Motivation can come in many forms – you can coerce, you can force, you can bribe. But what we really want to do is 'inspire' our kids. And there's only one way to do this, and that's by getting inside our kids and lighting a fire.*
>
> ~ Wally Amos

That's why having goals is so important. Goals come from within. They provide the fuel for the passion to learn. I think you're going to find that as your homeschooling becomes more fun you spend more time doing it and you get more accomplished, instead of forcing yourself to force the kids to do their homeschooling. Instead, you are approaching your day with, "What are we working on today? Where are you on your goals?" And then you just have fun working together, learning and growing as you go. You don't have to know everything ahead of time. You can explore together and make changes along the way. It's an exciting adventure.

♥ Confidence-Building Goals

You're not setting your future in stone. The point is to set goals in your mind and your child's mind, like goalposts, to have a sense of direction and purpose behind your studies. Having specific goals will motivate your children. You'll find them more interested in their studies, because suddenly learning is relevant to their future.

Oftentimes, the reason most kids don't assimilate information in schools is because it doesn't seem to pertain to what's most important to them. But if you get them to tell you what *is* most important to them—what they want to do in life—they get engaged in their curriculum. They're more invested in their own futures. Suddenly they're studying for themselves, not because they are being made to.

But what if they don't know what they want to do? Marilyn Mosley believes one of the best ways you can help your children visualize their path in life and their goals coming true is by actually seeing more of life itself. Expose them to many activities and a range of professions that they wouldn't normally have access to. We are limited by what we can and can't imagine, so expanding their vantage point expands their possibilities. She recommends:

Take a lot of field trips, such as going with your children to see ice-skaters, or going to a farm and working on the farm, visiting another city or town, learning about people and meeting with people. Read about people and create stories about children who are doing things in the world and learning about them and even interview them. Participate in activities such as volunteering. Try anything that will give the children a chance to activate a particular part of the brain that isn't usually activated in the normal circuit of their life. All these activities help to expand their thought processes and their preferences."

Some people are reluctant to set goals because they think, "What if I don't achieve them?" This is the old New Year's Resolution Syndrome—it's become so cliché to not follow through on New Year's Resolutions that we figure, why bother? But did you know that just the act of writing down your goals actually increases your chances of achieving them?

Again, you'll start with the big picture goals, then work your way down to your child's and your yearly, semester and daily goals. If you have a high school student, we will cover high school goal setting more in a later chapter to make sure that they are on schedule to pass their exams, graduate, and fulfill college application deadlines.

Remember, your kids don't have to know exactly what they want to be and do for the rest of their lives. This goal setting process is just a tool to help you start customizing your child's education so that they can go where they want to in life. It's okay to be flexible.

♥ But What If I Fail?

It's so important to teach our kids that there is no such thing as "failure," only results. That eliminates the shame and guilt and "I'm a big fat failure" equation that some kids can get caught up in.

If your child gets a result she doesn't want,
let her know it's okay to just try Plan B instead.
Believe me, I've had a lot of experience with plan B and I've discovered
oftentimes plan B ends up better than plan A.

In other words, it's okay to fail sometimes. If your child believes they set a goal and "failed" at it, reframe the situation for them so that it doesn't rob them of their precious self-esteem. Let them know that all great successes have been built on a foundation of previous failures. In fact, they are not "failures" at all, but simply steps to an end result or new conclusion, even when the conclusion might be, "I don't like that as much as I thought when I first started out."

Bobbi DePorter is the founder of SuperCamp and the author of *Quantum Learning.* When I interviewed her she talked about how "failures lead to success," saying:

I think it's an important change in mindset to look at our failures and instead look at them as gifts. What can we learn from them? What can we do with failure that will lead to our success? When we look at a failure as something that leads to success, we don't put ourselves down and say, "Oh, I failed once, I'll never be able to do it" or "I got a bad grade on this test and I'll never be any good in school." Instead, we change that around to: "Okay, I failed on that exam." Instead of telling yourself, "I'm too stupid I'll never make it through college," we tell ourselves, "I failed on this but I tried. So what can I learn from this to do better next time?"

Your kids will be changing, growing and discovering new information as they work on their goals. They might decide: 1) I don't want this goal any more; 2) I want to modify my goal to something else; or 3) I want to try this again later when I'm ready.

Sometimes "failing" might indicate that a child set challenging goals for herself that were perhaps a bit too difficult. If that's the case, stopping doesn't mean she's "giving up." Remind your child she was ambitious and confident enough to try it. If your child has a tendency to set goals that are a bit out of reach for her level, let her know it's good to stretch, but even if the idea "fails" it doesn't mean *she* is a failure. Simply scale back a bit on the next goal. Or let her keep trying as long as she doesn't let it damage her confidence level.

Letting your child set some personal goals will make your job as the teacher a lot easier and more rewarding for both of you. You get to be more creative. And they get to be more themselves, while pursuing those interests that are unique to them.

SUGGESTION BOX

What Other Homeschoolers Say About Goals...

"Regarding goal-setting, no matter what it is, make it a contest (beat the clock; do better than yesterday, who can finish first). With my child, I cannot let her know what the ultimate goal is. She has a hard time seeing the big picture. I have to break the goal down into bite-size pieces and give her a challenge to finish each bite. My goal may be to form a certain habit. Her goal is simply to successfully complete each small task either more quickly or more competently than ever before, which eventually gets her to the place that I want her to be."

"Our primary goal is to serve. So we approach each subject from the mindset of, 'How does learning the piano enable me to serve better?' 'How does learning my times table enable me to serve better?' 'How does learning to read and finding the main idea enable me to serve better?'"

"Decide what your child's goal is together. Preparing for a family, Bible college, trade school, etcetera? Then school accordingly. Do not be under needless pressures that are not in accordance with *your* goal."

"Homeschool from the heart! We were blessed that our daughter knew her 'purpose' early on. Her passions were evident. We have built her high school years around that. Yes, we still do the basics but they are constructed in a way that feed those passions and prepare her for those things she wants to spend her life doing. We also had her choose at least three plans for after high school (schools etc ...). We then made a list TOGETHER of the criteria needed for those, for example. entrance requirements, and audition requirements. From there, we built our curriculum plan. Not only is she not going to have any problems meeting her first college choice requirements but two of her other dreams have already come to fruition! She will be traveling overseas for the second time this summer as a missionary. She just got a job in the entertainment industry, at the company she wanted to work with! Next spring we will be traveling to London for her to audition at her college of choice. She is 15."

♥ Why Set Your Own Personal Goals as a Parent

Several years ago my big goal was to run a marathon, though I was not a runner by any stretch of the imagination. It was a huge confidence builder. I can tell you, in fact, that it was because of that marathon that I had the confidence to start Homeschool.com.

I remember in January I started with running one mile on the weekend, then the next weekend I would add another mile so I was up to two. I remember when I was running three I thought, "Oh my gosh, I never thought I could run three." The marathon is over twenty-six miles long and takes place in December. By October, I was behind schedule and I fearfully thought, "Oh my gosh, I'm not going to be able to do it." I was supposed to do a seventeen-mile run that day and I felt defeated and I told the kids that I couldn't do it. That I would have to quit. My children and their neighborhood friends wouldn't let me quit and were determined to help me. They came out with me and took shifts either running with me or riding a bike with me, while carrying my energy bars and giving me water. It was a terrific experience for everyone.

Creating goals together is team building. Parents and children supporting each other in their goals are saying, "Hey, I know you have a special purpose and talents and I'm here to support you in those."

Sometimes goals can be so big and scary that you don't even attempt them. When we were asked by Time Warner to write *Homeschooling for Success*, my first response was, "No, I don't have time for that." I was afraid it would take too much time away from my family. Fortunately my best friend caught me and said, "Are you kidding?! That's one of your before-I-die-goals. Of course you're going to make time for this!" I had this fear that I would become a bad mother or that our family life would suffer if I took the time to write a book. We only had twelve weeks to write twelve chapters, so it meant a lot of long days.

It ended up being wonderful. I wrote one chapter a week and then on the weekend I would celebrate with the kids. The goal was that if I had the chapter done by Friday, then we would go to Monterey, or out to dinner or do something special. That way, my children really participated in my goal. And now, of course, *they* all want to write books too.

If this is a book about homeschooling your child, why is it a good idea that you, as a parent, also make goal setting a habit? As a parent and teacher, if you are fulfilling your goals on a regular basis, you set a fantastic example for your children. Your personal goals matter. They help you keep your life's priorities balanced and make you a more organized and motivated homeschooler.

I have my own personal before-I-die... goals list and I try to make sure that I am achieving one of these goals each year. Last year it was to live in France. The year before that it was to tour New Zealand and Australia. This year I am working on writing this book. Next year I think I may want to drive cross-country or learn the guitar.

You want your children to see you working on your dreams and living life to its fullest. That way they will know that it is okay for them to follow their dreams too. This is role-model parenting at its finest.

Establishing a practice of regular goal setting will:
- ❤ Keep you both on track throughout your child's entire education
- ❤ Build your child's confidence as they see their ability to set and hit their own goals
- ❤ Prepare your child for a successful and rewarding life

When I interviewed Marilyn Mosley, I asked her, **"What about for the mother and father who don't really know what their purpose is yet? How can they help their children find theirs?"** She answered:

That's such a great question because it's so intrinsically important. The nice thing about homeschooling is that the parent is learning along with the child, so we're students together. As your child is developing he or her dream, parents has a chance to reconnect with their own dreams and find themselves. As you are encouraging your child, you as a parent can be encouraging yourself. Whether it's taking those dance classes that you never took or the bicycling tour that you never did or learning to write the book you wanted to write. As a child is getting in touch, so can a parent....I just feel that it is never too late to become who you really are, and all you need to do is take the step along with your child and to appreciate yourself.

Oftentimes when we're homeschooling, our focus is on making sure that our child has everything that he needs. It is really important for the parents, especially the moms, to make sure that they are being supported and nurtured as well, so that 1) they have the strength to support their child and 2) that they are becoming and developing their own interests, loves and talents. My children became some of my best supporters. They helped me really to develop my commitment to homeschooling, to start Laurel Springs School, to continue my dancing lessons, to lecture, to help write books. They became my support team and I became their support team. We understood that we were there to help each other. What happened was that we never developed a polarized relationship, we had a relationship that was built on trust and supporting each other's goals.

Our children want us to be successful. They want to support our successes. It's very reassuring for a child to see their parent growing and expanding. That's such a beautiful example of how our family is our support team. A support team of like-minded people is one of the greatest assets that anyone can have and you can have a support team of all ages. You invite people onto your team of all ages so that you don't have age segregation and you get the wisdom and the beauty of all these different people who are standing behind you supporting you to make a difference. It's all part of the modeling process.

We're so afraid sometimes that pursuing our own dream might seem selfish. But really, pursuing our dreams is role-model parenting.

♥ Set Semester Goals

The next thing you're going to do is work with your child to create semester goals. Now that you all know what your big dreams are, this idea is so simple and effective, it's funny that we don't do it more often. Simply ask your child,

"What do you want to learn about this semester?"

You will write down your children's goals at the beginning of the year or when they think of them, and then do everything in your power to help them achieve these goals. When my son wanted to write and publish his own sci-fi/fantasy novel, I found a writing coach for him who had experience in this area, and we shifted his class load so that he could make writing his top priority. Your child's goals will determine the way you set up the year's curriculum, so stay as creative and flexible as possible (while still staying efficient with your time and money). We'll cover all this in Chapter 5: Customize a Curriculum.

Failure-Proof Goal-Setting

Object of the Game: Make the impossible possible. Set it on paper, including the date by which it will occur.

♥ Step 1 - Write 100 Personal Life Goals

Stop what you are doing and get out a piece of paper. Write across the top *"Before I die, I want to…"* Then quickly write a list of the top 100 things you want to do, learn or see before you die. This may come easily to you or it may take awhile. It could be that no one has ever before asked you what you want. Oftentimes, we become so engrossed in what we *should* do that we don't give much thought to what we *want* to do.

You don't have to come up with 100 things on your list right off the bat. Just write down as many things as you can think of off the top of your head, then keep the list nearby so that you can add to it as you imagine new ones. You may see a movie or talk with someone or read a book and suddenly think, "That's a great idea. I want to add that to my list!" Once you start, the ideas just keep coming. You may even remember things you've always wanted to do, but had forgotten about.

To get you started, here are some of my before-I-die goals:

- ♥ Learn 5 languages
- ♥ Write a book
- ♥ Learn the guitar
- ♥ Travel to Africa, the Galapagos Islands, Easter Island
- ♥ See the aurora borealis

You get the idea. Just let me insert a word of caution here. In the beginning, you may want to keep your list private (except for your kids and maybe your spouse). When your dreams are new they are fragile and you don't want anyone's negativity to shut you down before you even give it a try. I hung my list on the inside of my closet door so that I could see it and be inspired by it, but I was careful not to confess my dreams to anyone who I thought might be a "dream killer."

I don't have to worry about this too much nowadays because I have a reputation for doing what I say I am going to do. And I have proven to myself that I can achieve my goals. But in the beginning, when you are just starting to set goals, you may want to share your goals only with people whom you know will be supportive of you. Sometimes it is the people you are closest to who can be the most negative. They love us just the way we are and they don't want us to change.

♥ Step 2 - Choose some goals you want to achieve this year

Before I established the habit of regularly setting goals for myself, I never seemed to get anything accomplished. I would start one thing and then change my mind and move on to something else. I set New Year's Resolutions, but I quickly forgot them. And I never really allowed myself to dream big, because I didn't trust myself to be able to pull it off. I thought it would be another failure or false start.

Then I discovered a simple goal-setting method created by Lynn Rose, creator of the "Goal Getter" and "Wow Factor" programs (www.LynnRose.com). I promise you, if you want to achieve ANY goal in your life, just follow these steps.

Decide what goal(s) you want to accomplish this year and write it down on an index card. In the beginning, you may want to choose only one goal and make it a goal that you are 80 to 90% sure you can accomplish. When you succeed at this goal it will build up your confidence and your track record. You become a person who does what you say you are going to do.

♥ Step 3 - Write each of your goals on an index card and post them where you can see them every day

The language you use when you write down your goals is very important. Here are three ways of writing them down that will make them more likely to occur:

1) Focus the statement on what you *do* want, not on what you *don't* want. For example, you don't want to say, "I don't want to be late anymore." Instead, you'd say, "I want to be on time." Add some positive feelings to your goal.

2) Write it in the present tense as if it's already happening.

3) Put a completion date on it. For example you might say:

> *"This December, my family and I will be off on a fabulous five-month trip to Africa. The kids are learning so much on this trip and our family is closer than ever because of this experience."*

"This semester will be our best semester ever. The kids are on fire – totally excited about what they are doing and what they are learning. This is the happiest our family has ever been and I am amazed by what they are learning."

"By June, or sooner, I will have completed my first novel. I am so excited. I have enjoyed every step of the way and the book is fabulous. I'm holding the finished book in my hands and I feel great! Colleges are going to LOVE me."

"My goal this semester is to get on pointe. I'm taking 10 hours of dance classes each week and before I know it my teacher will tell me that I am ready and that my legs and feet are incredibly strong."

"One of my goals this semester is to get volunteer hours by fostering little kittens and finding them good homes. I am really enjoying this and I feel I am making a difference by saving the kittens' lives and finding them great homes."

After you have written your goals on an index card, tape the card up on the wall or somewhere where you can see it every day. I like to tape mine to my bulletin board.

♥ Step 4 – Imagine experiencing yourself achieving your goal

First thing every morning, read your goal out loud and feel how wonderful it will be to accomplish that goal. Flood yourself with the good feelings you'll have while accomplishing what you set out to do. See yourself achieving that goal. This is what so many athletes do when they're running a race or playing a game—they literally imagine winning *before* they even start the game. The more you do this, the more comfortable you become with accomplishing your goal. What once seemed impossible will soon feel totally natural and inevitable.

♥ Step 5 - Take action every day on that goal

Even if it's just a baby step, make sure you take action every day toward your goal. If your goal is to get your driver's license, then every day you make yourself go out for a practice drive. If your goal is to write a book, then every day you take the time to write – even if it's only a few sentences. If your goal is to lose weight, then every day you take action by exercising, even if it's only for a few minutes. These baby steps add up and the momentum is incredible. Plus, this way you keep your goal fresh in your mind. Your action steps may be different every day, but the idea is to think about your goal and do something about it every day.

Let your children see you working on your goals every day. And show them that your top priority is helping them with their goals.

Now that you're working on your goals, next is an exercise that will help your children discover their goals – that will help them to think big, excite their imagination, and encourage them that they can do anything in life.

For you, the point will be to know your children's personal goals so that you can begin to design their curricula around accomplishing these goals.

Setting Life and Semester Goals

Object of the Game for Parents

Let your child know that everyone has a purpose in life. It's expressed through fulfilling their interests, talents and goals. Encourage them to let their imagination go free. The point is for them to know you support them in what they want to do and have confidence in their ability to achieve anything.

Object of the Game for Kids

Have fun imagining all the things you could do in your life.

♥ **Step 1 – Have your children write down up to 100 things they want to do, be, have, try, see, or make—next week, next year, or in their lifetimes.**

Now that you have created your own list, share your list with your children (maybe not all 100 at one time). You could share the most important life goals and then a few of your year's goals. Use this as an opportunity to talk about the importance of goal setting.

Once you've shown them your list, let them know you want them to create a list of goals of their own. They don't have to start in the same moment you introduce the idea to them. And it doesn't have to be 100—that's a lot for a child to imagine. They can add to this list for years to come. The idea is to encourage them to write down their goals and ideas as they think of them. Get used to validating them. You could arrange to take them out on a private goal-setting lunch or dinner or picnic, or as part of your school day.

Depending on the age of the children, you may not be able to ask them openly, what is your dream? What do you see yourself doing five years from now, or one year from now?

> *It doesn't usually work well to try to force a child to conceptualize a year or two down the road unless they are actually a competitive athlete, actress or actor who has a very clear, strong focus. There are few children who know exactly what they want to do for the rest of their lives when they're eight or ten. Instead, you can talk about how every person has a purpose in life. It lights up their eyes. It makes them so excited to know that they are special. Every child is unique and is here to do something that is very unique and special. As the parent, show your child you have confidence in his or her ability.*
>
> -- Marilyn Mosley

They may want to write down the list themselves or they may want to dictate the list to you. The list doesn't have to be in order of importance. Just write down their ideas in the *Custom Home Homeschooling Plan* at the back of this book. Those goals are different from their semester goals, which we'll do next. Semester goals will cover traditional subject areas like history, math and reading. For now, you just want to find out what your children are most interested in and what they are passionate about.

Remember: You don't have to know HOW you are going to make their goals come true. Right now, you are just going to listen carefully to what your child says and write down every goal they tell you.

You can call these "goals" or just "wants.". The object is to excite their imagination and get them thinking really, really big. This is not the time to say, "That's impossible" or "I don't think you can do that," or "Are you sure you want that?" Just let them have fun with it. If they get stuck, you can ask them:

- ♥ What activities look fun or interesting to you?
- ♥ What people do you want to meet?
- ♥ What would you like to do?
- ♥ What would you like to be?
- ♥ What would you like to have or see in your lifetime?

♥ Step 2 – Set semester goals

Okay, you've identified what your children are passionate about, and got them really opening up their minds to what's possible. Now it's time to flesh out their semester goals.

Have them decide what their #1 goal is. This may have nothing to do with "school." Then let them decide their specific goals for each subject. These will become their top priority for the coming semester. Your top priority will be to design your child's curriculum around accomplishing these goals.

Your children may choose from their list of 100 or they may just get more specific with what they want to study this semester. It could be to write a book, raise kittens, drive boats, etc.

My oldest daughter's goals last spring were:

- ✓ Be on time to every dance class
- ✓ Get straight As.

My son's goals were:

- ✓ Get his driver's license
- ✓ Turn in all of his homework on time
- ✓ Pass the AP exam
- ✓ Get a trophy from his table tennis club

My youngest daughter's only goal was:

- ✓ Start taking a dance class in January and stay with it all the way until the recital in June.

♥ Step 3 – Post their semester goals in their bedroom or in a workbook

Have your children write down or print out their goals, then put them where they will see them daily or at least weekly. You may also want to put a copy for you in a curriculum book, organizer or calendar. If there are steps you and your child need to take to achieve that goal, note in your calendar the dates by which you need to do that step.

CHAPTER FOUR

SAVE TIME, MONEY AND TEARS
by Teaching to Your Child's Strengths

♥ **Discover Your Child's Unique Learning Style**
♥ **Create Personality Profiles for You and Your Children**
♥ **Find Ways to Teach to Their Strengths**

As homeschoolers, we have the advantage that we can identify how our children are smart and how they learn best, and we can customize and tailor their education to suit their needs and their strengths. No wonder homeschooling is so successful, and homeschool children are doing so well academically as well as socially.

When I was first starting out, our homeschooling was very boring for my children and very difficult for me. As I mentioned earlier, I knew the subjects themselves were actually interesting, but I made it harder for all of us by thinking I had to teach them in a certain way. We all sat at the kitchen table, we kept a strict schedule, I used the same standard curriculum for all of them. Essentially, they could have just gone to school!

When I finally got around to asking my children what was most important to them, what they wanted to be, do and have in their lives, I made an interesting discovery having to do with learning styles and curriculum. I noticed that when my daughter spoke about her goals and what she wanted to learn, she also naturally told me *how* she wanted to learn.

She told me she didn't want to do a science fair project (she wanted to do science kits), she did want to take an online math program, and she wanted to write a huge report. What I discovered from this information was that her particular personality type is called a "Producer/Planner," according to a system that we'll cover later in this chapter. The way she described her likes and dislikes fit the Producer/Planner profile well.

It suddenly made sense to me why she was losing interest in a subject I knew she loved. The way I was presenting it was better suited to her brother's style of learning. He is a Deep Thinker and an audio learner. I'm an audio learner too, so I naturally teach my children by talking to them. But my daughter is a visual learner and therefore she needs to read in order to understand.

Isn't it interesting…

When we ask our children what they want to learn, their answers naturally reflect their individual learning styles.

♥ Eight Different Kinds of Smart

Most parents and teachers, I've found, believe that "learning styles" refers only to whether or not a child is an audio, visual, or kinesthetic learner. These are actually learning "modalities." Learning styles encompass much more than modalities. "Learning style" takes into account your child's learning personality and unique talents, interests, and favorite activities -- even the environment in which your child learns best.

You have probably also heard the idea of multiple types of intelligences, such as "emotional intelligence." David Lazear is somewhat of an anthropologist. He's traveled all over the world studying the way different cultures think, do tasks, and conceive of the world. Along with Howard Gardner, who did a lot of the neuro-brain science behind multiple intelligences, Lazear developed a list called "8 Different Kinds of Smart." The list categorizes how we tap into our potential by using all of the ways that the mind integrates information. The idea is that we all have each one of these smarts, but some are more latent than others. We just need to be creative in the way we apply our strengths to make up for our "weaknesses," -- or I should say, subjects that don't come as naturally to us or to our child. Let's take a quick look at each of these "smarts" one at a time.

Here are the different ways we can assimilate information:

1. **Visual-spatial intelligence, or** *Image-smart*
2. **Bodily-kinesthetic, or** *Body-smart*
3. **Logical-mathematical intelligence, or** *Logic-smart*
4. **Naturalist intelligence, or** *Nature-smart*
5. **Musical rhythmic intelligence, or** *Sound-smart*
6. **Verbal linguistic, or** *Word-smart*
7. **Interpersonal intelligence, or** *People-smart*
8. **Intrapersonal, or** *Self-smart*

Here is an excerpt from an interview I did with David Lazear called, **"8 Different Kinds of Smart."** As you read, be thinking about which one best describes you and your children.

David Lazear: *The intelligences, the way I look at them, are bio-neurological cognitive ways that we process information. Ways that we come at understanding, ways that we come at learning, ways that we know what we know in our lives. I believe that everybody has all eight intelligences, but some of them are more dominant. The key is to figure out how we can awaken these and develop them in our lives. When you get out in the big world, beyond schooling, in your adult life, you're going to need them all.*

*1) The first intelligence is visual-spatial. I call this **Image-smart**. This is really the ability to use visual representations, active imagination, and mental imagery to solve problems and understand information. These are the children that if you draw them a picture, or if you say let's go inside our heads and pretend, they instantly understand.*

*2) Next is bodily-kinesthetic. I call this one **Body-smart**. This is the intelligence that uses physical movement and performance. This is what many educators talk about as learning by doing. It uses movement and learning-by-doing to solve problems and understand information.*

*3) Another is logical-mathematical. I just call this one **Logic-smart**. It's really the capacity to analyze problems logically, to carry out mathematical operations, and to detect patterns, to reason deductively and to think logically.*

*4) **Nature-smart**. This is the most recent one that Gardner identified. He's called it the naturalist. This is really just the whole area of understanding the natural world, knowing how to use it appropriately, how to conserve its resources, how to live off the land. I think probably one of the best examples of Nature-smart are the native people really of any country of our world. You think of the Native Americans, they had a very profound and deep understanding and appreciation for the earth. In fact the earth was almost like a sacred alive entity that informed them that they knew how to understand the patterns of nature.*

*5) Musical-rhythmic intelligence; this one I call **Sound-smart**. This has really nothing or little to do with what we usually call musical ability. It's really much more about dealing with a whole realm of sounds; sensitivity to sounds, and rhythms, tones, beats and vibrations. It's the ability to create music and rhythm to express oneself and to aid in memory. This is a very, very powerful intelligence.*

*6) **Word-smart**. Gardner called this one verbal-linguistic intelligence. Word smart is really all about sensitivity to the written and spoken language; the ability to use language to express oneself and to help one remember information. Word-smart and logic-smart are the big ones that are most valued in our schools. And if you are good in those and do well in those areas, everyone thinks you are really smart. If you don't, then you get labeled as something else.*

*7) Interpersonal. I've called it **People-smart**. This really involves the capacities of person-to-person relating, teamwork, communication, and collaboration with others. These are the kids who, when you tell them what you want them to do, they need to discuss it before they can actually do it. They need to talk with one of their peers, or talk with a sibling. They are people who do well with team-oriented tasks.*

*8) Intrapersonal intelligence. I call this one **Self-smart**. It's really understanding oneself and one's feelings, having an effective image of oneself and being able to use that image to regulate ones own life. It's much more the introspective intelligence. Where we are raising the big question, the purpose, the significance, the value, raising the who-am-I question, what's-it-all-about questions. That's where self esteem develops -- when we look at ourselves and begin to understand and appreciate ourselves and we can present that self in social situations.*

***People-smart** and **Self-smart** are really two sides to a single coin. They are very, very hard to separate from each other because things we know about ourselves, we also know about other people. When we are working with other people we often learn things about ourselves. They kind of flip-flop back and forth -- two sides to a single coin.*

We have got to change the bias of our current curricula which almost exclusively values a verbal-linguistic and logical-mathematical intelligence. So it's a matter of imbedding the capacities of the different intelligences into the design of curricular units so that students have ample opportunities to practice using them to gain knowledge, process information and deepen their understanding of the required material. You simply look at the material you're going to be teaching and you start making links with the different capacities and you use those capacities to help students process the information you're teaching.

Author: *I have a nephew who is a nature-smart child. He is happiest when he is outdoors, when he's camping. If he were dropped off in the woods somewhere, he could survive. He's having a very hard time in his English class. In fact, he had to take summer school, and it's starting to damage his self-esteem. He's starting to think of himself as not smart. How can we help him reframe this image so that he can succeed better in school? How can we advise him in how to use that smart for his future?*

David Lazear: *Probably the first thing that I would do is say, "Let's get him into the outdoors." Work on helping him create a language for himself related to the natural world; to weather patterns, to animals, to all of the natural stuff that he likes. I would start there, helping him go back and forth between his*

appreciation of nature and how he can write about that, how he can explain that, how he can communicate that to someone else.

For homeschoolers -- or any parent or educator -- the idea is to identify how your child is smart so that he or she can use that strength to learn. If your child is People-smart, then let her learn in a group. If your child is Body-smart, let him learn by moving and using his body.

♥ Personality Types

Mariaemma Willis is another expert on learning styles. Her learning styles profile, I believe, is one of the best. It is located at: http://www.learningsuccessinstitute.com/products.html   According to Mariaemma, when it comes to personality types, there are 5 different learning personalities:

1) **The Performer**—Needs to move, craves variety, is a risk taker. She or he tends to be competitive and likes an audience. Oftentimes this child is labeled as hyperactive. The performer is also often a hands-on learner and may become an entrepreneur.

2) **The Producer**—Likes to plan, and tends to be project oriented, logical and orderly. This child likes workbooks and structure. This is the type of learner who does very well in a typical school setting.

3) **The Inventor**—Asks lots of questions. This child is a builder and he or she learns by making connections or associations in their mind easily. For example, when you are studying Egypt and you ask the inventor what she is thinking about, she might answer, "jewelry." It might seem illogical if you didn't realize she had made progressive connections from Egypt to pharaohs to mummies to tombs to treasure to jewelry. Inventors are often labeled as ADD and can do poorly in school because they are imagining so far beyond the next question in the workbook. They are already relating the information to the larger world picture. They are probably the most misunderstood, but can potentially grow up to be an Einstein or an Edison.

4) **The Inspirer**—Wants win-win relationships so tends to focus his or her attention on people. This is the caring, sensitive child who likes harmony and working in teams.

5) **The Thinking Creative**—A deep thinker who focuses on the ramifications of the information just learned, or on one particular aspect of it. Children with this personality type may be better able to express their creative interpretation of a lesson, rather than its details. Many become artists, musicians, or writers.

As you read through these descriptions, did any of them remind you of one of your children? Take a minute now and think about how each of your children approaches life. Which learning personality fits each one best? My youngest daughter is a Producer, my oldest daughter is a Performer and my son is a Thinking Creative.

What about you? Did you recognize yourself in any of those descriptions? As you read through these next sections, think about your own strengths and styles too, so that you can figure out a way to best use them to support your child's growth.

The more you know about personality types, learning modalities, talents, interests, and preferred environments—the more you can develop ideas for teaching in ways that best support both of you. The information you get may also help explain why you may find it easier to teach one child than another, perhaps because you share similar styles. As you continue to teach, you may also notice different aspects of your children's personality that alter your approach to how you teach them.

♥ Discover Your Child's Unique Learning Style

I knew a parent who said of her child, "If she sings, she remembers it forever." Now this could mean she is a Performer personality. It could also indicate that she is an auditory learner (which is a type of learning modality), or that she is Sound-smart. These systems are helpful to understanding your child. Learning how your child learns best will make the child more successful. After all, our job is to bring out a child's interests and talents. To honor children's needs, organize your homeschool so that they work in the location and in the way that works best for them. We'll cover this in more detail in the next chapter, when you customize your child's curriculum. But be thinking now about how all of this new information relates to how you're going to teach.

Learning modalities describe what senses people tend to use more than others to process information. Within each of the three learning modalities, there are two different types of learners.

Visual learners tend to take in more information by *looking*. One type of visual learner learns best from *print* (such as from reading). The other type of visual learner absorbs information through *pictures*. (from videos, pictorial histories, websites, etc.).

Auditory learners tend to take in more information by *listening*. One type learns best by listening to others (lectures, audio programs, etc.). The other auditory learner takes in information by *talking to themselves or others (*repeating out loud information they read, teaching others, dialoging, or hearing themselves say it in their own minds).

Kinesthetic/tactile learners tend to take in more information by *feeling*. One type learns best by *moving their whole body* (acting things out, touching, interacting and experiencing things in a tactile way). The other type of kinesthetic learner takes in information by *moving their hands* (sketching, writing, making a model, etc.).

According to Mariaemma Willis, most people use a combination of learning styles. She believes that we don't use the same style for all subjects. For example, a child may be more auditory for history, but pictures work best in math. Maybe for facts and information you like to hear it, but for math you're a picture learner. To learn maps, maybe you need to draw them.

Here's an inspiring success story about how you can use an auditory learning style within a visual memorization technique. It comes from an interview I did with Bobbi DePorter, creator of SuperCamp for kids and the Quantum Learning program. She has lots of great techniques for better note-taking, reading, writing, memorization and more on her websites at: www.supercamp.com and www.quantumlearning.com.

Bobbi DePorter: *Memory is about being specific with content and creating pictures in our mind and making associations. When we make those connections and associations, that's learning. We do have the potential to be a genius and we can remember so many things when we get really specific about it. We want to picture things and then associate things together. For me, the most important part is to be specific. In our minds, we tend to be loose with our pictures and we don't connect specifics. There are all kinds of mnemonic or memory techniques, from storytelling to linking things to location, to peg systems, and those are all things I would encourage people to delve into. It builds confidence. My son went to SuperCamp and learned these memory strategies. He had gotten a 66 on the SAT on the verbal part, so he used these mnemonics to create pictures and associations with vocabulary, and he got 99.9% after this. He almost aced this verbal part AFTER two days of memory skills. Now he is a parent and my granddaughter came home and my son told me that she had to learn all 50 states with their names by the shape on a map. This is not her style, she's not very spatial, she is auditory, and she couldn't get it and she said, "Oh I'm never going to get it and every student in the class knows I'm the only one that can't get it."*

My son took her aside and took the shapes and they created a story for each shape. She knew a movie, it was Napoleon Dynamite, and there was a tether ball in there and they are from Idaho so she looked at the shape of Idaho (it has this kind of smoke stack that goes up) and she pictured a tether ball on it. She made these associations; 'Napolean, he's from Idaho.' She went through every state and created a story. Her teacher had been trying to teach her this for two weeks and all she did was burst out into tears. Here my son spent 10 minutes with her and when she went to take the test, when the test came up, she was the first child (the only child) to get all 50 and she did it in the shortest amount of time and she was laughing because they were silly stories and shapes and she knew all 50 of them.

I have created a simple learning styles quiz and have included it later in this chapter, but here's a quick and easy way to identify your child's learning style, just through observation.

Closely observe your children this week. What are they naturally drawn to? For example, my son loves audio books and he can listen to them for hours on end. I love audio books too, but my daughters find them annoying. My son and oldest daughter are both good with their hands. They love using Sculpey clay and my son used to love Transformers, Legos, and K'Nex. I'm lousy with my hands. I'm not artistic, I don't cook (at least I don't want to cook), and I don't knit or sew. But I read two to three books a week and I like anything having to do with business and marketing.

What are your children's strengths? What are they drawn to? Do you have a child who loves to play the piano or some other musical instrument? Do you have a child who is gifted at sports and is happiest when outdoors or moving around? My husband is a very visual learner and I am a very auditory learner. When I was in college and I was having a hard time understanding a textbook, I would read to myself out loud. I didn't know why I did that. I just knew it helped. And when my husband and I were first married, I would have these grand ideas and I would excitedly try to verbally explain them to him, but he couldn't "see" them. So I learned to put my ideas down on paper in bullet points so that he could understand what I was talking about. Do you get the idea? Learning styles tend to be pretty obvious and they really aren't that big of a deal -- except when it comes to the kinesthetic learner.

We live in a mostly visual and auditory world, so you will have to think outside the box to support kinesthetic learner. Teach them to trust themselves and to pay attention to how they learn best. Do they learn better if they are pacing the room? Do they have lots of opportunities to get their energy out? If you are not a hands-on learner, then you might automatically think that your child will learn well through workbooks or movies, but what they really need are hands-on projects and kits. Teachers in a classroom can't really have each child working on separate kits. It's too time-consuming and messy. But homeschoolers can. When I asked our Homeschool.com Product Testers what three changes they would make to their homeschooling, many said that they would add more projects and more field-trips. These are great for all types of learners.

Okay, it's time to include this information in the Custom Home Learning Plan at the back of this book. Think back to how your children talked about their goals. That's why I had you record the dialog -- because their language will reveal a lot about their learning modality. If you have a kinesthetic learner, did he or she naturally include a lot of moving around or field trips or hands-on projects as part of his/her goals?

Isn't it interesting...
...Every child has a completely unique way of learning.
Finding your child's "type" will help you design a curriculum
that makes learning—and teaching—much simpler and more effective.

♥ Talents and Interests

Before I knew any of these distinctions, I remember that from a young age my daughter tended to move like a dancer. Even when she played softball, she looked like a ballerina rounding the bases. And now she *is* a dancer. My youngest daughter always seems to be writing, and her favorite gift was a beautiful journal. She's still young and I don't know where this will lead, but I'm making a mental note that writing may be one of her special gifts. I want to be aware of any fun ways that I can help her develop that talent. I used to think that music was one of her gifts. She played piano all the time, but now she's suddenly lost interest. I'm not forcing her to stay with it, but I'm betting (and hoping) that if I make some neat opportunities available (and don't force things) that she will come back to music. I'm not sure what my son's "smarts" are yet. When he was little he built things all the time. He doesn't do that anymore -- either because we haven't made those opportunities available to him or because he's outgrown out of that stage. One trait that has stayed with him is his sensitivity and kindness. These pieces of information may have a bearing on his career or college choices later on.

I asked **Marilyn Mosley,** "How young can you start to have your child understand what his own skills are?" She answered: *"You can actually begin dialoging with children when they are in kindergarten or first grade. Work with them on it, and then by the time they're in third grade, they will be capable of making decisions and working with you side by side. They'll be able to help you with the process. It can be a really simple conversation. At the beginning, simply acknowledge when they express an interest in something, then affirm and express your appreciation of their talents.*

In some people, passions, gifts and smarts are more obvious than in others. I had a childhood friend who knew when she was 12 that she wanted to be a singer and actress, and she's never strayed from that path. She has accomplished that goal. I was more of a generalist – pretty good at a lot of things, but not great at any one thing. I make sure that I work in an environment where I have a lot of variety and where being able to do several different things well is a strength.

Talents and interests are usually related. That's fortunate, because if a child is talented for algebra, for example, he or she will probably also enjoy that subject. Your child's talents may become obvious when you see what subjects and activities she enjoys or shows great interest in. However, challenges can arise when a child is interested in one area -- like becoming a singer, for example -- but does not have a natural talent for it. What if your child says she wants to be a doctor, but she's not strong in the sciences?

It's important to realize…

> **A child can overcome almost any obstacle
> with a strong enough interest.**

That's why it's important to learn your child's talents and interests. If they match with their goals, great. If not, you and your child may need to do some extra work to build the skills she needs to reach her goal.

♥ Learning Environment

When you are determining your child's unique learning style, you also want to find out what environment suits him best. You may discover that one child likes a lot of structure and another needs a lot of freedom. And perhaps one child needs longer transitions between tasks than another. Some like the ritual of having a daily schedule and knowing what to expect. Another child may find this to constricting. My oldest daughter easily jumps in and tries new things. My son is more cautious and it helps if I describe to him what's going to happen before it happens.

This week, notice:
- Where do your children do their best work?
- Do they like quiet? Or do they like to have music on in the background while studying?
- Are they alone in their room? Or working with the family around the table?
- Do they concentrate better sitting still or moving around?

♥ Teaching Styles

Your next assignment is to create personality profiles for you and each one of your children. What does your own learning style have to do with anything, if you're the teacher? This is where *what* you teach and *how* you teach start to come together. You will really appreciate having this information later when you are designing a curriculum for each of your children. Also, if a child is ever having difficulties with a certain subject, you can always refer to your child's learning style to help you brainstorm new approaches to teaching it.

ACTIVITY

Create Student & Teacher Profiles

Object of the Game
To understand your children better
so that you can teach more effectively.

♥ **Step 1 – Write down YOUR own Personality Type and Learning Style**

Go back and read the section on personality types if you need to refresh your memory. Did you recognize your own learning style in those descriptions? Does it match the way you feel most comfortable teaching?

Q: What is your personality type? Are you a Performer, a Producer, an Inventor, an Inspirer, or a Thinking Creative? Do you tend to teach predominantly as one type?
A:_____

Q: What is your dominant learning style? Are you auditory, visual or kinesthetic? Do you find that you tend to teach to that style?
A:_____

Q: What are your strengths and passions?
A:_____

Q: Environment: How and where do you work best?
A:_____

Q: How do you teach best? What are your particular strengths?
A:_____
A:_____
A:_____

♥ Step 2 - Write down your CHILDREN'S personality type and learning style.

What are your children's personality types? Which "smarts" do they seem to be demonstrating? Really pay attention to these and remember them for the future. One of these may become your child's passion and gift – and may help your child make career choices.

If you're not sure which one best fits them, write down a few possibilities. They may demonstrate some traits from one type, then others, when they are studying a different subject.

Q: Write down the name of each of your children. What do you think his or her primary learning style is? Is one style particularly dominant? Or do your children seem to show more of a blending of styles?

Name: _____ Style:_____
Name: _____ Style:_____
Name: _____ Style:_____

Q: If you have a kinesthetic learner, what changes can you make in your curriculum and schedule to help that child?
A: _____

Q: Regarding the "8 Kinds of Smart," write down each of your children's names. Which "smarts" does each seem to demonstrate?

Name: _____ Smarts: _____
Name: _____ Smarts: _____
Name: _____ Smarts: _____

♥ Step 3 - Write down the 5 things that you are best at

I have to admit I had a very hard time coming up with my own list. When I was first asked to write this list, I couldn't think of anything that I was good at. I could have written 50 things that I was bad at, but it was almost impossible to come up with 5 things that I was good at. Isn't that sad? This is why it is so important for our children to start thinking about what they are good at now, while they are still young. They may change or add to their list as they grow older. The important thing is that they begin to recognize their strengths. One of the best ways to succeed in life is to make sure you are in situations where you get to use your special talents.

- ♥ What are your particular talents and interests?
- ♥ What do you have a gift for?
- ♥ What do people compliment you on? For example, if someone says, "You are so good at that. You may it look easy," write that down.
- ♥ What are you really passionate about?

If someone ever says, "You are so good at that. You make it look easy," write that down. These are the things that you are probably best at.

Q: Write down the five things that YOU are best at.

1._____
2._____
3 _____
4._____
5._____

Q: Now ask your children what they think THEY are best at? Each child should make a personal list.

1._____
2._____
3 _____
4._____
5._____

♥ **Step 4 - Write down your child's best learning environment.**

Some people prefer to be in a new environment everyday. Others concentrate better when they sit in the same chair at the same time each day. Think about what suits you best when you're teaching. Then think: Do your children tend to like some areas better than others? Have you noticed where they are when they seem to integrate information the best?

Q: Where do your children learn best?
A: _____

♥ **Step 5 – Using each child's learning profile, brainstorm ways he or she could learn each subject.**

There is plenty of room here to get creative!

_____
_____
_____
_____
_____
_____
_____
_____
_____

Make sure you've made enough copies of the
***Custom Home Learning Plan* at the back of the book.**
Each child should have his or her own learning plan.

ACTIVITY

My Best Learning Styles

Object of the Game
Make learning easier!

♥ **Step 1 – Share your own profile with your children.**
   Explain the object of the game...
   to make learning easier.

Go to the copies that you made of your child's *Custom Home Learning Plan* where it says **My Best Learning Styles.** Explain that everyone has different ways of learning the same information. None are better or worse than another, just unique. This way, *you* can find out the best way to teach to your children's strengths, and *they* can develop their strengths and really shine!

♥ **Step 2 – Take the Learning Styles Quiz on the next page.**

Learning Styles Quiz

Here's an easy Learning Styles/Learning Personality quiz for you and your children to take. (Each person should do his or her own quiz).

First, let's identify your primary learning "modality." Circle the one answer that MOST describes you.

1. Are you good with your hands?
c) yes   d) no

2. Do you enjoy listening to audio books (books-on-tape)?
a) yes   d) no

3. How do you learn best?
a) I learn best by listening
b) I learn best by reading
c) I learn best by touching or building things

4. I am very aware of, and sensitive to, the sounds around me.
a) yes   d) no

5. I am very aware of, and sensitive to, the visual details around me. I notice what people around me are wearing. I notice little details.
b) yes   d) no

6. I like to move around. Sometimes I think best if I can pace or tap my pencil or wiggle my legs.
c) yes   d) no

7. I love to read. The more books the better.
b) yes   d) no

8. When I really want someone to understand me…
a) I talk to them about it
b) I write my idea down on paper

9. I do NOT do well in a classroom setting.
c) True. Classrooms don't work that well for me.
d) False. I can sit still just fine.

10. I am a natural athlete.
c) yes   d) not really

11. When I was younger, people thought I was "hyperactive."
c) yes   d) no

12. When I get something new, I almost always read the directions.
b) yes   d) no

13. I tend to hum and/or sing to myself.
a) yes   d) no

14. I love to write (letters, journals, etc).
b) yes   d) no

15. I can talk on the phone for a very long time.
a) yes   d) no

Score your answers.

Let's see if there is a learning modality that you are particularly strong or weak in. Count the number of a) answers that you had. Then count the number of b) and c) answers. Record these below.

a = Auditory	_____	(number of "a" answers)
b = Visual	_____	(number of "b" answers)
c = Kinesthetic	_____	(number of "c" answers)
d = "no" answers		(no need to count these)

_____   Write your style here: A, B or C.

Based on this quiz, what is your primary learning style (modality)?

_____

Analyzing the Results

Most likely, you instinctively already know what learning modality you are and what modality your child is. Audio and visual learners usually do well in school. Sometimes kinesthetic learners do not do as well. Most people are a combination of all three modalities. The purpose of this quiz is to help you identify if there is one particular modality in which you are really strong so that you can use that strength.

You can use this self-knowledge to help you communicate with others. For example, you might say to others:

> *"I find that I remember best if I can write things down. Do you mind if I take notes while we talk?"*

> *Or,*

> *"I seem to think best if I can talk out my ideas. Can I brainstorm my ideas with you for a minute?"*

> *Or,*

> *"I'm a hands-on learner. I need to be able to move around and use my hands as much as possible."*

People also have a tendency to teach to their own learning modality. This is why you want to know your own learning modality as well as the modality for each of your children. This way, you can adjust your approach. For example:

- If your child is a strong kinesthetic learner, give him plenty of opportunities to build things, move around, and use his hands.

- If your child is strongly visual, then you want to keep the learning lectures to a minimum and instead give her lots of written materials.

- If your child is strongly auditory, then give him lots of opportunities to listen to books and to tell you what he has learned.

- Bear in mind, that most young children are kinesthetic learners and need as many hands-on projects and kits as you can give them.

♥ Step 3 – Have your child answer these questions

If your children feel they need some help figuring out their learning styles, here are some questions that might help guide them. Ask these questions, and have them fill out their answers in their Custom Home Learning Plan.

Personality Types

- What do you feel you are good at?
- What do you enjoy doing the most?
- Say, "I see you… _____ (for example, "…writing a lot." Or "reading a lot") "Do you think this might be one of your special gifts?"

Talents and Interests

Write down your children's special talents—the top 5 things your kids say they are best at. Remind them why this list is important: They will be able to be their best when they are using their natural talents to their fullest. You can always tell them what you notice they are great at. You can also ask them:

- What do you think you're naturally good at?
- What do you really enjoy doing?
- What are your favorite subjects?
- Has anyone ever ask, "Wow, how do you do that?" What was that talent?
- What are your particular talents and interests?
- What do you have a gift for?
- What do people compliment you on?

Best Learning Environment

As they're filling out their Custom Home Learning Plan, ask questions like:

- Where do you do your best work? At the kitchen table? In your room? On your bed with the door closed?
- Do you work better alone or with others?
- Do you like quiet? Or do you listen to background music?
- Do you concentrate better alone in your room? Or with the family, sitting around the table?
- Do you concentrate better sitting still or moving around?

CHAPTER FIVE

CUSTOMIZE A CURRICULUM
....For Each Child

- ♥ **Develop Goals for Each Subject**
- ♥ **Develop This Semester's Curriculum**
- ♥ **Find Teaching Materials, Classes and Tutors to Fit Your Budget**

So far, you've accomplished the following:

1) You know *what* kinds of things your child wants to achieve overall
2) You know *how* they learn best

Now it's time for you and your child to decide *which* subject goals they want to achieve this semester and put together a curriculum that best supports each child's learning styles and goals.

Remember, the whole point of the goal-setting exercise in chapter three is to make education relevant and personal for your children. By customizing their learning plans, you can make their education be about attaining their dreams and wishes. You can design their curricula around accomplishing their goals, using their unique strengths. When they help you customize their plans, they take more responsibility for their learning. They own it. Instead of pushing them through it, you can simply be their guide and inspiration.

Sounds like a tall order, I know. Especially when you have more than one child and you've just discovered they all have different learning modalities, like my three kids! Well, here's where homeschooling actually gets to be even more fun. You'll be teaching to your child's strengths. You get to be creative, and your child gets to be more accountable for his or her own learning. You'll both find this is a whole lot easier than trying to cram information into your child's memory bank. By supporting each child in this way, you are saving yourself a lot of time, money and tears. You will be teaching with heart.

♥ Set Goals Within Each Subject

Have your children get more specific about what they want to achieve within each subject area. They can write this down themselves, within their own copy of the Custom Home Learning Plan, or you can do it together as a dialog. If they're having difficulty prioritizing, figure out what's most important to them by asking specific questions. For example, here's the dialog I had with my 11-year-old daughter.

Q: What is your math goal for this semester?

A: I want to take an online math program like my brother took last semester, with a real teacher and regular class times.

Q: Why?

A: Because it will be like real school and I don't want to do math by myself this year.

Q: What is your reading goal for this semester? For example, do you want to read a certain number of books? Or read a certain amount each day? Or read a certain type of books?

A: I want to do the library's reading contest. If I read 30 hours I can get four coupons and two prizes.

Q: What is your writing goal for this semester?

A: To win four more writing contests and to earn a prize of $100.

Q: What is your science goal for this semester? What would you like to study? For example, do you want to learn about volcanoes, dinosaurs, earthquakes, or the human body? Do you want to do science experiments each week, or work on one project at a time? Do you want to research a special topic and write a huge report?

A: I want to learn about tornadoes, avalanches, tsunamis, earthquakes, and volcanic eruptions (natural disasters). I want to find a web site that shows videos of these things. And I want to do some science kits and labs with you, especially a weather experiment. I don't want to do a science fair.

Q: What is your history goal for this semester? What would you like to learn about?

A: I want to learn more about 1776, and also about President George W. Bush and the next election. Will a woman win? I also want to learn about England during the time of *Pride & Prejudice*. And I want to write a monster report about England.

Q: Is there anything else special that you want to learn about? Is there anything special you want to do for art or music or dance or foreign language?

A: I want to learn more French and German. I want to take care of different animals at the same time, not just a kitten. For example: tigers, zebras, pandas, monkeys, skunks, mountain lions, and raccoons.

I loved the answers my daughter gave me. She felt very listened to and I learned a lot about her. I would never have come up with these goals for her on my own. With goals like these, can you see how homeschooling is going to be so much fun? Isn't it great that they are going to be learning what they need to learn, but in a way that interests them?

♥ Cost Considerations

While you were reading through this, did you hear a cash register pinging in the background? I want to comfort you about money right away. Homeschooling can cost a lot or a little. It can cost as much as you want it to cost.

It is possible to be creative and cost-effective at the same time.

I spent very little on homeschooling during my children's younger years, but I am discovering that it is costing us more to homeschool my high schooler because now he is taking more classes, working with tutors and coaches, and participating in exciting summer programs. I'm okay with that and I am budgeting for that because for us, education is a top priority. I justify the expense by telling myself that we are giving him a fabulous education for far less than it would cost to send him to a private school.

If you add together the anticipated costs for all of your children and find they are too high, you can go back and find a less expensive way of reaching that goal. And because you have planned ahead, you have a better chance of staying within budget. It's okay to combine projects for children of different ages. It saves time and money. It also gives them a chance to learn from each other. For example, my high schooler and grade schooler are taking French lessons from the same tutor at the same time. They also work on unit studies projects together, each at his or her own level and in the area of personal interest.

For other cost savings, the easiest way to find bargains on school supplies and learning materials is to go to Homeschool.com and look through our Resource Guide (www.Homeschool.com/resources). Lots of new and used materials can be found at your local homeschooling conventions and curriculum fairs.

♥ How to Teach Children of Different Ages at the Same Time (Even with a baby or toddler in the house!)

If you have a baby in the house, congratulations. I'm so jealous! My "baby" is already 11 and I miss those wonderful, hectic baby years. As you create a curriculum for each child, you will want to be thinking of ways you can combine activities. Having a baby around the house doesn't have to interfere too much with helping your other children fulfill their goals.

If you have a baby or toddler and you can arrange for your spouse, older child or caretaker to help out while you are homeschooling, then that obviously makes things easier. If you don't have that option, you may want to work around the baby's schedule and do your one-on-one homeschooling when the baby is napping. Be kind to yourself and be flexible. This is a wonderful time for everyone, and your older children are lucky to be able to spend so much time with the new baby. Other kids have to go off to school, but you get to spend time bonding and creating memories as a family.

When there's a toddler in the house, the goal is to keep your Tasmanian Devil busy doing fun stuff so that you can work with your older children. One of the best ways to do this is to create a box or basket filled with fun activities that get to be used only during your school time. This will keep the goodies fresh and exciting and special, and will keep your toddler occupied so that you can work with your other children.

If you have a toddler, your homework assignment is to put together a special homeschooling box or basket just for them. You may also want to have some educational videos and educational software programs on hand that you can use to keep one child busy while you work with another.

Toddler Learning Basket

- ☐ Stickers
- ☐ Coloring books
- ☐ Crayons
- ☐ A wipe-off board
- ☐ Special books
- ☐ Worksheets to color
- ☐ Toys that are used only during homeschooling times

When coming up with your semester's curriculum, be thinking of ways you can combine projects and lessons—to save you both time and money.

On the next page, I've included some great ideas from other experienced homeschoolers on how to homeschool children of different ages at the same time.

Suggestion Box

"We use a rotation system. I have three children aged 12, 10 and 7 and while I'm working with one, the other two are either working together on flashcards, playing an  *educational game or having free time. I combine lessons as much as possible. It's amazing what the younger ones pick up from the older kids' lessons. We do a lot of reading aloud; we again use a rotation system with each of us each reading a chapter."*

"When my children were all small, I would homeschool the oldest while the babies were napping. Any toddlers had a box of fun toys and such that was taken out only during school time. Now that all my children are teens, my solution has been a home satellite program with each of them having their own taped classes. That leaves time for my youngest to have my whole attention. The others bring their work for me to check after they are done."

"Sometimes toddlers just want to be like the big kids and will sit and do 'worksheets' like the big kids at the table. Sometimes we will 'read a story' and they don't care if it is out of a science book that their brother is reading, as long as it has pictures and is read with excitement. Sometimes a baby is just happy that everyone is on the floor with them. Just have a clipboard for the kids that are writing. If the kids are learning the same subject, the younger ones benefit because they will pick up some of the more complicated stuff from the older child's subject matter. I like playing games, board or question games. The kids can play together even when they are different ages. We'll let them pick another card if they haven't learned that yet, or one of the older kids will answer it if they know. Then, if that question comes up again, the younger ones might remember the answer."

"We actually teach and work in separate rooms when it comes to the different ages. While I may be working on a task with one, the other is doing some independent learning."

"I have a basket of toys, books, crayons, etc for the two-year-old to do 'school' while we do. I get down on the floor to teach so that the little ones can gather around me and color or whatever they are doing, and I am still accessible to the older ones for questions about subjects. We have also taken to doing more of a unit study approach with as many subjects as we can, and use hands-on activities that the 'littles' can do as well."

"I set out an agenda that has me rotating between each child and the toddler. The older children rotate between time with mom, working independently and occupying the toddler."

"I will find something to occupy my youngest, such as flour or rice in a container that he can drive his cars through, or paint, or markers on the dry-erase board."

"I try to keep special 'fun' books for the little ones that they can use only during 'school' time. I also work around naps, etc. I read aloud to all of them while I rock the little ones. That way we're still getting in our reading. Some days I do have to resort to bribing with a treat or two!"

"I teach up to the highest child's level. Our oldest is now 19 and in college, our youngest is 10. Math in particular... our middle child yesterday needed help with polynomials and how to find the greatest common factor, so we sat the youngest down and asked her to listen and participate, but to not worry whether she 'gets it' or not because this will simply reinforce the information when it's her time to learn it."

"I find something for each of them to do that they enjoy. Whether it is my toddler coloring pictures on the coffee table while my oldest reads a story aloud to me, or getting out the puzzles for my younger grade leveled child to work on while my infant is in her baby swing, enjoying her binkie and listening to my oldest child's story as well. I include schoolwork for all of them in one way or another while tending to my infant while they are doing their work."

"Homeschooling different age children isn't a problem. I give my children a list of what is expected of them that day, week, month, etc. and they are in charge of finishing the items on the list. My husband and I are available to help them when they need assistance. We are also blessed in that our youngest son is a morning person and our oldest is a night owl, so we rarely have them begging for help at the same time."

Get Creative, Brainstorm Ideas

Now that you know what your children's goals are, it's time to figure out how they are going to accomplish these goals. Start by reviewing their big-picture goals: what they want to accomplish in their lives. Then, define their semester goals and then look at how you can do those goals within each subject. Get resourceful. Be sure to include your child in this process so that he or she will know how to reach future goals on their own.

Using the earlier example for my daughter, I'm going to show you the progress of a Semester Curriculum for which I brainstormed ways to fulfill her goals and her brother's and sister's goals all at the same time, sometimes combining them to save time and money. On a piece of paper I typed my child's name and her top semester goal. Then, I went subject by subject and wrote down what she said she wanted to learn in that area.

After that, I brainstormed some curriculum ideas and wrote those down too (see below). You will write down your own curriculum in the Custom Home Learning Plan.

Here's what my curriculum looked like…

NAME: Madison (age 11)   DATE: These goals are for 6th grade, fall semester.

Madison's #1 Goal: "I want to pick out a kitten from the Animal Shelter, raise it gently and train it for awhile, then find it a good home. I want to save its life. I also want to work with wild animals like tigers, pandas, lions, raccoons, etc."

Curriculum Idea = Her brother needs volunteer hours for high school and is interested in working at our local nature center. What type of wild animals do they work with? We have mountain lions and wild turkeys and skunks in our area. Will this count for Madison's goal? If so, then perhaps she can volunteer there too. If not, then perhaps the Nature Center can recommend where she can go to work with tigers, lions, etc. Perhaps the zoo in our area?

COST: _____

Math Goal: "To take an online math program like my brother took last semester, with a real teacher and regular class times."

Curriculum Idea = I have found an online tutor who will work with her one on one, using a special white-board technology. I'll have to ask the teacher what textbook she likes to use for pre-algebra. And I want Madison to talk with the teacher on the phone to make sure my daughter likes her and wants to work with her.

COST: _____

Reading Goal: "I want to do the library's reading contest. If I read 30 hours I can get four coupons and two prizes."

Curriculum Idea = Unfortunately, I believe the library's reading contest only takes place only in the summer. But they are very nice, so perhaps we can adapt their program and they'll save some of their coupons and prizes for her. I will also work with Madison to create a specific list of the books she wants to read, encouraging her to read a variety of books and to include a couple on the list that might be challenging for her. We can tape a sheet to the fridge where she can keep track of her reading time.

COST: _____

Writing Goal: "To win four more writing contests and to earn a prize of $100."

Curriculum Idea = We'll use Homeschool.com's "Contests and Scholarships" list for this at:
http://www.homeschool.com/Homeschool_Contests_And_Scholorships/default.asp . I'll ask her how she wants to do this; Does she want to apply to 4 to 6 contests all at once? Or does she want to do one contest a week?

COST: _____

Science Goal: "I want to learn about tornadoes, avalanches, tsunamis, earthquakes, and volcanic eruptions (natural disasters). I want to find a website that shows videos of these things. And I want to do some science kits and labs with you, especially a weather experiment. I don't want to do a science fair."

Curriculum Idea = I will sit down at the computer with her and find some good sites that show videos of natural disasters. Maybe there are some DVDs that we can rent. I was thinking of asking her to show me what she learns from this by putting something together on a big board, but since she specifically said she doesn't want to do a science fair, perhaps it's best to just learn this for enjoyment's sake and not make a big project out of it. Or maybe ask her if she wants to print out photos of some of these and put them into a report. I'll ask her what she wants to do. Maybe she'll want to use this topic for the giant 3D project that I'm going to ask her to do. (I talk more about this later in this chapter). For the weather kit, she and I can do a Google search for home science kits and see if there is anything she wants to order.

COST: _____

History Goal: "I want to learn more about 1776 and President George W. Bush and the next election. Will a woman win? I want to learn about England during the time of *Pride & Prejudice*. I want to write a monster report about England."

Curriculum Idea = We already own the movie 1776, so we can watch that together and discuss it as we go. Her brother also wants to follow the presidential election, so perhaps we can specifically talk about this during our family dinners. Maybe her brother can present to us something new he has learned. Madison likes to read the paper, so perhaps she can cut out articles for her brother to read. Her brother also wants to learn more about the war in Iraq, so maybe Madison can cut out articles about that, too. Will she want to tape these on a wall somewhere? For Pride & Prejudice, *we already own the DVD so we can watch that together. We can also watch* Sense & Sensibility *and* Emma. *Her brother studied* Pride & Prejudice *for AP Lit last year, so I can ask him to teach her what he learned. That'll reinforce his learning too. Since she wants to write a giant report about England, does she want this to be a written report, or does she want England to be the subject of her giant 3D project?*

COST: _____

Art Goal: No specific goal at this time

Music Goal: No specific goal at this time

P.E. Goal: No specific goal at this time, but she may occasionally go with her father and brother to their table tennis club and she'll continue to play at home.

Foreign Language: "I want to learn more French and German."

Curriculum Idea = This is her brother's goal, too, and I have found a wonderful tutor who will come to our home once a week. She has all of her own supplies and teaches using textbooks, conversation and movies. She sounds expensive, but worth it.

COST = _____

Chores: Taking care of pets, keeping her bedroom tidy, and taking care of her daily hygiene.

Goals That I (the Mom) Want to Add to Her List:

1) I want the family to take a First Aid / CPR class together.

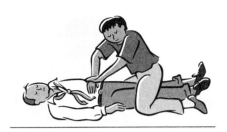

Curriculum Idea = I will call the Red Cross and our local parks & recreation office to see if they have any classes.

COST = _____

2) Although Madison did not have a specific dance goal, I am going to encourage her to audition for the Junior Dance Company and see if she wants to try it for the semester.

Curriculum Idea = We will stay with our local dance studio. They're great.

COST = _____

3) I want to plan time with Madison every day to do some type of craft or kit.

Curriculum Idea = Michael's sells a lot of neat kits from Creativity for Kids. We'll go to the store and buy 5 to 10 kits that she is interested in. I'll store these in the art section of our bookcase and she can choose which one she wants us to work on.

COST = _____

4) I want to teach all the kids how to cook this semester. I want them to know how to make an American Thanksgiving dinner, and I want them to know how to make 6 different dinners, 3 different breakfasts, 3 lunches, and a unique specialty meal that they are really proud of (maybe something from another country).

Curriculum Idea = We already have a bunch of cookbooks, but the kids might also like to check out some new ones from the library.

COST = _____

5) I want to add a special 3D project for all my kids. (See the next page for details)

Curriculum Idea = One of Homeschool.com's Product Testers wrote in about this and I thought it was a great idea. Directions for how to do your own 3-D project are coming up next.

COST = _____

Now it's your turn to get creative! (And, still keep an eye on costs).
After I typed up my curriculum ideas, I printed out this sheet for Madison and taped it to her bedroom door to keep it fresh in both of our minds. The next week, I created a football chart for our fridge and each member of the family chose one goal that they were going to work on. We also bought some craft kits.

You may discover, when asking your children what they want to learn this semester, that some of their goals are the same. For example, both of my children wanted to learn about the upcoming presidential election, so my youngest is going to look through the papers and cut out articles on both the election and the war for her big brother. Both kids are interested in weather, so we'll do a weather kit together. For volunteering, both kids are interested in working with animals so I will see if they can volunteer at the same place and at the same time.

Is there some way you can combine your children's goals or have them work together so that teaching them easier for you?

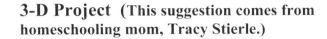

3-D Project (This suggestion comes from homeschooling mom, Tracy Stierle.)

"I have always tried to give my children some outlet for their personal style, so we incorporate at least one multimedia project into their curriculum per year. This allows for their personality to shine through on the topic of their choice and in the presentation of their choice. And, it provides a break from the more tedious 'three R's' -- (Reading, wRiting, and aRithmetic). We do these projects with the final goal being the State Homeschool Convention Student Expo, where they compete for ribbons and prizes. But even without participation in an expo, these projects are great showpieces and confidence builders.

"The key for us is to begin the process early -- identify their subject of interest and brainstorm about presentation. Most often these projects would take the form of a trifold project board, and they would incorporate all sorts of items that were inviting to the observer -- bubble-type stickers, sandpaper, small objects that could be hot-glued to the board (starfish, shells, miniature items that correlated with their subject, personal photos, etc.). It had to include as much original artwork as possible, and the information had to be handwritten, not just printed off the Internet. This is where their personalities could shine. The work becomes fun, as it is a treasure hunt of sorts to come up with interesting items to include. My daughter was unsure of a topic for this particular year, so we decided on salmon -- a very important natural resource to our area, and a great subject that covers science, history, art, Native American studies, and more.

"Her interest was sparked when we decided that a liberal use of glitter to highlight her subjects would be eye-catching, and she really embraced the project, coming up with lots of ideas to present the information with bling! My middle son chose helicopters and used a model helicopter glued to the board as somewhat of a centerpiece, used a pop-out approach to present historical information, and created a visual of a city all along the bottom of the board with helicopters in the air above. He visited a local airport, and the proprietor of a helicopter company was delighted to show him around the hangar. He educated my son about the copters and let him take pictures of the different models. Both children won Grand Champion ribbons at this year's convention, after winning both Grand Champion and Reserve Champion ribbons for the previous year. These projects take several months to complete and are a great source of pride for them. The key is to take time, let your imagination go wild and try to create something that is as much fun to read as it was to create. The final project should invite the reader to touch it and explore and want to spend time on each section."

Suggestion Box...more!

♥ What Other Homeschoolers Say About Creating a Curriculum

"My daughter has always loved to cook and create in the kitchen. She asked me if there were cooking schools for children and, luckily, there are. The one in our area even offered homeschool classes! Not only does she LOVE the classes, but her reading has improved dramatically."

"This year I am trying something new. We are utilizing our public library once a week extensively to research and explore topics that are interesting to our girls. For example, our 2nd grader has an interest in Celtic music, so we found a video on Dublin. I am trying to keep the learning environment going in a fun way, so I am listening to what the girls are talking about and subtly introducing materials to them that will educate them without stressing them out. And we drive a lot, so I borrowed an audio Spanish program from a friend and we are using it as we drive or sit in traffic."

"My daughter and I made a flip chart for our Summer Homeschool Plan. We hung 5 teacup hooks under the edge of our kitchen counter. We then cut out 5 brightly colored ovals, decorated one side with stickers, and punched a hole near the top so that we could hang them on the teacup hooks. On the non-decorated side of the ovals, we wrote a school-related activity, such as: 'Journal: Write 3 or more complete sentences,' and 'Reading: Read to someone for 15 minutes or more.' We also included 15 minutes of physical activity which could be anything of my daughter's choosing such as taking the dog for a walk, going for a bike ride, practicing gymnastics, or swimming. We also included an oval for 15 minutes of music practice. My personal favorite oval is the 'Mom's Choice' oval. This card allows me to slip in whatever activity I think is important to my daughter's education. So far, I've included math practice sheets, a trip to the library, some science experiments, logic worksheets, educational games, and even some local volunteer activities. Each morning I place the oval cards on the teacup hooks so that the writing side is facing out. My daughter has until 7:00 PM to complete each activity. If she doesn't complete them by 7:00 PM, she is not allowed to swim (her favorite activity) the next day. She can complete the activities in any order and at any time. When she completes each activity, she turns the oval card so that the decorated side is facing out. With a quick glance into the kitchen, I can quickly see which activities my daughter has completed or still needs to complete."

ACTIVITY

♥ Customize Your Semester Curriculum

Before we create your curriculum, I want to make sure that you are solid about your own goals and your children's goals. Take a minute to answer the questions below. This will ensure that you are moving in the direction you really want to go.

♥ **Step 1** – Keep in mind your child's life goals. Sometimes, as homeschoolers, we get mired in the everyday details and lose sight of the big picture. And we just need reminding that homeschooling is not a chore but an honor. Education is not drudgery; it is a lifelong discovery.

Q: What did you discover about your child's goals?

_____

The goals your children set are important. Be sure to keep them in mind. Reaching for these goals is when your children are really going to shine and when they will probably be happiest.

Q: What did you discover about your own goals? What are you best at?

_____   _____   _____

Q. What do you hope to achieve by homeschooling your children? "Our major goal in homeschooling is to teach our children..."

_____   _____   _____

"I will consider our homeschooling a success if my children grow up to..."

_____
_____
_____

Try to make sure that you yourself are working with your strengths and interests. And encourage your children to use their special talents too. Let your children see you working toward your goals.

♥ **Step 2** – Do the Setting Subject Goals exercise with each of your children separately.

Speak with each of your children and ask them what they want to learn and do for each subject area. Keeping the big picture in mind, what baby steps will you be taking this semester to get there? The first step is to write out a goal sheet (like the one I included in the Custom Home Learning Plan at the back of this book) for each of your children within each subject—what they want to accomplish in English, in science, in math, etc. Or you can just write down some quick ideas here.

Subject: _____   Goal:_____
Subject: _____   Goal:_____
Subject: _____   Goal:_____
Subject: _____   Goal:_____

You'll notice that at the bottom of my daughter's goal sheet (as described earlier in this chapter) I added in some additional goals that I thought were important. For example, I really want the family to take CPR & First Aid, I want the kids to learn how to cook. Are there any goals that YOU want to add to your child's list? Perhaps some gaps in their learning that you want to fill in? Now's your chance!

Q: What goals do you want to add to your child's goal sheet?

_____   _____   _____

♥ **Step 3** – Brainstorm ideas on how they can fulfill each subject goal.

Now, you're the Homeschooling Research & Development Department. Isn't this fun? (Give yourself a raise! Or at least a pat on the back.) Refer to the learning modalities information in chapter four, think about what teaching materials and environments would work best to accomplish those subject goals. Write down some general ideas about where you can get the information you need.

For now, just write down your ideas. Then you can get more specific and find the exact kit, website, tutor, or book that you will need. Ask yourself whether there is some way you can combine your children's goals or have them work together so that it makes things easier for you.

_____
_____
_____
_____
_____
_____

♥ **Step 4 -** Start your research.

Make phone calls, use the Internet, or just use your imagination.

Here's the fun and the good news: You don't have to get everything done right away. Now that you know what your children want to do, and you have a general idea regarding the curriculum you'll use, you can just enjoy working on these goals a little at a time. You don't have to order a complete curriculum and make sure that it arrives before you can start. Instead, you're going to build your curriculum as you go.

And your children will gain valuable skills from this whole process. They will know how to set a goal, how to find out who or what can help them achieve that goal, and then how to take action toward that goal. They are going to be very much ahead of the game when it comes to succeeding in life. They are going to know how to research and find out about anything that they want to learn. They are on the path to becoming lifelong learners. And isn't that what you really want for your children? You won't be passively pouring information into their heads and hoping that some of it sticks. Their learning will be meaningful and exciting -- for them and for you.

♥ **Step 5 -** Create a way for them to gauge their progress.

This great idea came from Jack Canfield when I interviewed him about "Success Principles," available on Homeschool.com. He said that for his family, they like to tape a big piece of paper to the fridge that has a football goalpost drawn at the top. He then cuts out little footballs and the kids write one of their goals on each paper football. Whenever they make progress or take action toward their goal, they move the football up on the paper. When they achieve their goal, the football crosses over the goalpost and they celebrate.

For example, if your daughter's goal is to read ten books this semester, then every time she finishes a book, she would move her football a little bit closer to the goal. If your child wants to win some sort of musical or sports competition, then every time they practice for that event, they get to move the football closer to the goal. This is a particularly nice way to celebrate the little steps we take that make any big goal doable..

CHAPTER SIX

GET ORGANIZED!

- ♥ **Streamline Your System**
- ♥ **Stay on Top of Teaching Materials and Supplies**
- ♥ **Sell What You Don't Need**

"The benefit of being organized is that you can focus more and not be distracted by the environment. You also gain peace of mind because you have calmed a lot of the chaos that takes place every day."

~ Elizabeth Hagen, Professional Organizer and Speaker

I must confess that I am not by nature an organized person. In fact, a friend of mine once humorously suggested that I seemed to have a "high tolerance for chaos." I'm not sure what gave her that idea. At the time, one child was playing the piano, one was potting plants on the kitchen counter for a growing experiment, and our youngest child was out on the patio, painting with her feet. The microscope was on the kitchen table, and books were strewn on the coffee table. Everything looked normal to me!

In our house, there is always something going on and more likely than not, there are extra children running around too. And that's just the way we like it. But I do hate wasting time looking for things and I find it peacefully comforting when things are tidy and organized. On the one hand, a tolerance for chaos is a gift because I don't lose my mind when the kids do messy art and science projects. On the other hand, a chaotic workspace has wasted time and energy as I searched for scissors, workbooks, and teaching materials that I knew I had purchased…but I couldn't find! Often, by the time I found the missing workbook or art kit, the moment had passed and the kids were on to something else.

Nobody needs that kind of frustration. You don't want little naggy things, like not being able to find something, sapping your energy. That's what motivated me to become a lot more organized over the years. It was for my own peace of mind and so I could focus on what matters most to me—my children getting the best education possible.

I contacted three organization and time management experts -- Cheryl Carter, Elizabeth Hagen, and Sunny Schlenger -- and asked them for their advice for the contents of these next two chapters.

♥ Streamlining Your System

Are you a curriculum junkie who likes to collect new project material, but then you never use it? Are you one of those people for whom a school supply store is like your candy store? Do you have books and kits and workbooks scattered all over the place and can't find what you want when you need it? Or are you one of those people who can't bear to throw anything away…just in case you might someday use it? If these scenarios sound familiar to you, it's time to use these supplies, sell them, give them away, or trash them. You'll be amazed at how much more at peace you feel.

Getting rid of junk and getting organized is a great way to prepare for a new semester or a new school year. No more scavenger hunts around the house for supplies.

Some children don't learn well in a chaotic environment. Ask how your kids feel. Maybe it makes them uncomfortable or easily distracted or frustrated when they can't find their learning materials. That will detract from their effectiveness as a student.

Clearing out your garage, office or learning space can also clear a space in your head to be a more effective teacher. The goal here is not just to be organized for the sake of having color-coordinated stacks of things in neat piles. Being organized is a tool that allows you to accomplish what you want to accomplish. According to organization expert Elizabeth Hagen...

"Clutter is anything you own, possess or do, that does not enhance your life on a regular basis."

The exceptions to this, according to Elizabeth, are those special items like your wedding dress or the baby blanket that is in storage. This definition alone really helped me when it came to making decisions about what to keep and what to toss or give away.

A very similar definition can be used when getting rid of *time clutter*, which includes any activities that don't enhance your life. In the next chapter on organizing your time, we'll use Elizabeth Hagen's system for ranking your activities and getting rid of the activities that have the lowest ranking.

Remember, in chapter two we talked about how having a grander purpose helps you stay motivated? Well, it turns out that having another purpose— other than being organized—helps you to stay organized!

Here's a helpful perspective from homeschooling organization expert Cheryl Carter...

"You should not have a goal to 'get organized.'
Getting organized is a step to a bigger goal; perhaps to start a new business,
have more time to read, etc."

In other words, if you tell yourself you should be more organized, that is not where you're going to find incentive. Instead, when you're looking at your messy house, feeling overwhelmed and asking yourself, "Why should I even bother?" think of this:

Clutter costs us:
- ♥ Time – spent looking for things
- ♥ Energy – both physical and emotional
- ♥ Money – we sometimes buy duplicates because we can't find the original
- ♥ Peace of Mind – we worry that others might see the clutter

The ability to have some time to focus on you, having more energy for yourself and a chance to work on the things you want to do personally, is a great incentive. This should help you find the bigger purpose behind doing this next exercise. By clearing up clutter, you will gain time and energy for yourself, and perhaps save some cash in the process. Organization expert Sunny Schlenger thinks of organizing the house in this way:

**"You can't give back something unless you take care of yourself.
It doesn't take away, it adds to, what we're able to give."**

That really turns it around, doesn't it?

♥ Where Do You Start?

So where should you start? Cheryl Carter suggests that you start by honestly evaluating how you use each room in your home. At the root of the word *homeschool* is the reality that your home (or at least part of it) is being used for a second purpose. And if, like many homeschoolers, you also work from your home, then your home is being used for three purposes. Clutter, disorganization and chaos can often become the norm, instead of the exception.

Organization experts agree that the key to gaining control is to formulate a plan that meets your specific needs, to work with what you have, and to organize around your homeschool and lifestyle.

An individualized approach is best for ensuring long-term change and adaptation because you're more flexible when you're more aware of what your strengths and weaknesses are. -- Sunny Schlenger of Suncoach.com, and author of *How To Be Organized In Spite Of Yourself.*

Cheryl Carter, Executive Director of *Organize Your Life* --
Homeschoolers have a lot going on in their homes; working, eating, living, schooling. To adjust for that, you need to make your home more purposeful for you. Purpose precedes order.

This means that you need to know the purpose of something before you can organize it. To apply this to a home, every room in the house has to be purposed for the activities that occur in that particular area. How do you honestly use each room in your house? The exercise at the end of this chapter will help you allocate supply space, living space and working space.

♥ Staying on Top of Teaching Materials and Supplies

If you're feeling any sense of overwhelm, remember, the goal right now is not to get your entire home organized and perfect. The top priority right now is only school supplies. Anything else you do after organizing the school supplies is icing on the cake. You also don't need to become one of those perpetually super organized people. You just need to organize your homeschooling supplies so that you can do a better job homeschooling. Then, ideally, you can come up with your own unique maintenance system for staying on top of teaching materials that works for you and your family. It's as simple as that. As a bonus, you may also find that you save money and save time, so you can get more accomplished, have less stress, and do more fun projects with the kids.

If you don't tend toward being super-organized, don't worry. This just means you may want to schedule time to organize on some regular basis, before things get out of control. If you are kicking yourself for wasting money on unused curricula, then stop right there. Being a homeschooler is a learning process in itself. What works for one child doesn't work for another. And something that looks awesome on the store shelf may turn out to be terrifically boring when you get it home. If you buy something and it doesn't work out like you thought it would, you probably just shelved it, thinking someone else would use it…and they still might if you do the Scavenger Hunt for Supplies Game (at the end of this chapter). But meanwhile, isn't it pretty neat that you are attracted to school supplies in the first place? Doesn't that say something about you and your love of learning? Think what a great role model you are being for your children. They see you excited about books and workbooks and kits of all sorts. How awesome is that?

By organizing your supplies, you're taking the first step toward organizing your time. When all your project and teaching materials are in one place, you won't be wasting time running around looking for them. In the activity page at the end of this chapter, I've given you a simplified way to organize your supplies. Remember, no two families are alike, and what works for one family may not work for another. Trust your intuition. Go for the system that feels best to you. There is no right or wrong. And be prepared to improve your initial organizing system as you go along.

Here are some examples of how other homeschooling families got resourceful and organized their educational supplies their own way. Be creative. Take what I am giving you and modify it to make it your own. Then write your ideas down right away before you forget.

SUGGESTION BOX

"We each, including Mom, have a notebook with calendars, lesson plans, lists, and dividers for work done. We have taken one wall in the garage where we have shelving. On these shelves we group together games, resources, and, in baskets, we have our school supplies. Everything has a place! Our children use a CD-ROM curriculum, and these programs have a section where I can easily see work done, work to do, a calendar, lesson plans, ideas, resource lists, grades and more. It's all laid out for both teacher and student."

"We have a school room with nothing but our school supplies in it. My husband took plywood and built into the wall two free standing desks on each side of my desk and two sets of bookshelves, one for each child. They hardly use their desks, but at least the room is organized. For me, organization is everything. My daughter and I are both dyslexic, so this works best for us. I have a separate bookshelf for all their fun reading and they have a cork board above their desk to display their art work, etc. I have a tall Rubbermaid closet that has many individual containers that we keep locked away from my toddler. It contains all of the small items and art supplies that must be asked for. I have a bin for each child that they can carry up and down the stairs for those times when we don't want to study in our classroom. I also keep the room locked so that they have to ask me permission when they want to retrieve a game, etc. This works well for us and keeps everything in its proper place and I'm much less stressed. Less-stressed mom equals happier kids."

"Our school supplies fit into a Tupperware bin with a lid. I keep the markers and colored pencils in their original case but crayons always seem to get mismatched so we keep them in a Cool Whip container. We have a desk area in our basement and that is where we do most of our studies. We found a desk at Office Max that is very long – long enough for two to sit at, with plenty of space. There is a hutch above with lots of storage space so that everything stays nice and organized. One side is for my daughter and the other side is for my son. Everything stays down here on the desk, other than books for reading that we take with us."

"I have a filing cabinet for each grade. This keeps all of my files organized by grade and each child gets a filing drawer, and I get a drawer for the records I need to keep for the school district. We use our dining room for our studies, so my filing cabinets are kept in the dining room and the books are in the hallway."

"We are a homeschooling family with 11 children and this will be our 16th year. We have lots of bookshelves and 2 two-door metal cabinets. The cabinets hold bins with art supplies and the stuff that no one knows where to put. Our latest shelving addition is a shelving unit from Sams' Club that has four rows with 4 small plastic bins. We keep our basic supplies in the bins, along with notebook paper, folders, flashcards, math manipulatives, etc. We put this in a closet that we opened up under the stairs. We have two older computers that go on one long folding table and some smaller tables and inexpensive desks for each of the kids. I have a big old wooden teacher's desk, and lots of one-on-one schooling is done here."

"We keep all of our kids' current schoolbooks together on a specific shelf. That way each child knows where their schoolbooks are, where to put them away and where to find them when they need them. We also organize our books according to subject matter, like history, science, etc. We use desk organizers that I found at a local teacher supply store to make sure that each child has a ready supply of colored pencils, pens, erasers, scissors, stapler, and hole punch. We keep our library books in a large basket, and this has helped us avoid quite a few late fees because now the library books are always kept in one location."

"Our books are kept all over the place, so I keep a list in a loose-leaf binder of everything we have. Each grade has a separate sheet of paper, so now all I have to do is consult my list to see what I have and what I may need to buy."

"I have a closet where all my homeschooling supplies are kept. I have my curriculum arranged as to school year so I can easily see what I have and what my needs are. My girls know where to find things and where to look. I also keep their records, such as grades, in the closet, so I can put my hands on them quickly. Their portfolios are kept in boxes by child and by year and then stored in the shed."

♥ Selling What You Don't Need

These days, there are a lot of ways to resell things. That's a pretty interesting educational project in its own right. A child can learn to navigate the Internet, create postings on Craigslist and eBay, and follow through with the procedures of selling online, which is fast becoming the way of doing business.

An older child can also research other options. For example, does your local homeschooling group have a used curriculum fair where your family can have a booth? Could you set up a garage sale? Or do you just want to be done with it and donate everything to your local library or thrift store? Some of us find it hard to give away books, but if you have a lot that are just taking up space, and are in good condition, consider a local bookstore. If they have a used books section (and even Barnes & Noble buys used books), take them over there, neatly boxed. They will inspect them one by one. You may get a financial return on each one, especially if they're classics or academic books in mint condition.

♥ Scavenger Hunt for Supplies

Okay, are you ready to get organized? This activity is actually pretty fun. Did you ever go on scavenger hunts in your neighborhood as a party game? Children would go from home to home rounding up a list of random objects. Well, now you'll be looking all over the  house for your supplies. The object of the game though is not "whoever has the most wins." The object is to end up with only what you need, then organize that stuff in one area so that everyone in the house knows where it is and can get it when they need it.

Most of us procrastinate when it comes to organizing. But even for a Master of Chaos like me, this assignment can be fun. For any packrats who have a hard time getting rid of stuff, the key is:

Don't keep anything out of guilt. If it is missing parts, throw it away.
There's a 99% chance that you are never going to use it.

As you do this exercise, don't do what I tend to do and hop from one project to the next. Whatever you do, do NOT put things back into storage boxes. By the end of the day, everything you need for your homeschooling should be easily accessible. Scavenger hunts are fun, but you shouldn't have to be hunting down what you need every day. I want you to be able to run your homeschool feeling totally organized, on top of things and with a light heart. I don't want you to add any more items to your to-do list. So it's really important that you try to set aside the time to do this activity all at one time. If that's not possible, schedule a time to complete each step.

ACTIVITY

Operation: Supplies Central (for parents and kids)

♥ Step 1 – Prepare one central place to keep all your supplies.

First, decide in what area of the house you want to keep all your supplies. You may need to buy a bookcase (or clear off a bookcase that you already have), or even clear one part of a room—office, garage, playroom, dining room, kitchen. When my children were younger, we used to store all of our supplies in some white cabinets that we purchased from Home Depot. I put these cabinets in our covered patio, which is where the kids did their messier projects. We organized this room into "centers" so in one area we had our science center, and in another we had our art center. We also had a bulletin board and an old table to work on.

How do YOU honestly use each room in YOUR house? Do you have a spot in your home for all your supplies? Do you tend to use one room more than any other? If so, then you might want to choose that room for storing your supplies. My children are older now and we don't have as many supplies, so we're just using a couple of bookcases. Decide what will work best for you.

♥ Step 2 - Gather all your materials and supplies in one spot.

Here's the scavenging part. If you are like most homeschoolers, your supplies could be anywhere. I found boxes of supplies in the garage, and I found art supplies in almost every room of the house. They were in game cupboards, in the kids' bookshelves, in a box under my daughter's bed...

Define the purpose of each room. For instance, if there are toys in every room, then there is no set place to play. Try to create practical rooms with items placed where you usually use them and where they work the best for you. Some rooms can be multipurpose -- you just want to be sure you have a system for moving from one activity to the next.

Look in every nook and cranny of your home. Once you've finished hunting, bring all those boxes over to your bookcase or storage area.

Cheryl Carter, suggests, "Go through the house the way it is now and ask yourself the purpose of each room and what activities are happening there. Be sure you focus not on what you want it to be but what the room is actually used for."

♥ **Step 3 – Sort your supplies into "Keep," "Dump," "Give Away" and "Sell" Piles.**

Set up a sorting station, in an area of the house with enough room for all of you to sit and make decisions about your collected "stuff." Bring with you:

- A large trash bag
- Empty bags or boxes that you can use for your thrift store donations
- A box where you will put things you want to give your friends (bring a pen and some sticky notes, too, so you can label these)
- If you want to try selling some of your things on eBay or Craigslist, then also bring a box in which you can put the items you want to sell.

Label each container according to what you're going to do with it: "Keep," "Dump," "Give Away" or "Sell."

Once you bring all your trash bags and boxes over to your bookcase area, you are not allowed to leave that area -- because if you leave you may never come back, and then you'll be stuck with a big fat mess (and your spouse will hate me). Think of this as homeschooling boot camp.

Go through each of the items you found and decide whether you are going to keep it or not. If you do keep it, then put it in your bookcase. Group your art supplies, science supplies, and math or history books together in their own areas. Trust your feelings on what to keep and what not to keep. If you love it, then keep it. If you don't love it, then pass it on to someone else who might.

♥ Step 4 – Find the perfect place for everything you decided to keep.

Do you have your math materials grouped together? All your science supplies in the same area? My 11-year-old made up labels for each of these areas and our bookcases now look like a well-organized library. It's peaceful to look at them and I get so many lesson plan ideas just by having everything handy and ready to use at a moment's notice. Plus, by having the bookshelves labeled, there's a higher chance that things will get put back into the right place. Everything has a home now.

Will you need another bookcase? I did. I found enough half-used pen art kits to fill an entire bookshelf. While you were doing this exercise, did your children find some long-lost treasures? Pay attention to what each child is drawn to. You'll find yet another clue to identifying their learning style. Hint: These are the types of supplies to use when designing their curriculum to their strengths.

Organization Expert Tip: Keep all pens, pencils, crayons, scissors, tape, etc in a box that fits on your bookshelf. The key here is that if someone wants even one item then they have to take the entire box. This way you'll have a better chance that the item will get put back into the box and that the box will actually get put back on the shelf. Pretty simple, isn't it?

♥ Step 5 – Get rid of everything else.

After this last step, you probably still have a mess on the floor in "Dump," "Sell" and "Give Away" piles. "Dump" is easy—just make sure it's really not anything you can recycle by giving to another family. If it is truly trash, then make sure any recyclable materials like cardboard or certain plastics go in the proper recycling bin.

Delegate who is going to handle the rest. The "Give Away" pile could go to other homeschooling families or to your local Goodwill or Salvation Army. Is there a local hospital, woman's shelter, toy drive or library that will take them? Or do you have older children who might enjoy trying to sell your "Sell" pile on eBay or Craigslist?

♥ Step 6 – Revel in being so well-organized!

Did you come up with a whole new system to keep things this organized all the time? Write your ideas down while you're feeling inspired, schedule a time to make it happen -- or even better, just do it now!

CHAPTER SEVEN

MANAGE YOUR TIME...
...Without Losing Your Mind!

- ♥ Learn the Easy 4-Step Time Management Plan
- ♥ Set Up Your Yearly Calendar
- ♥ Plan Each Week
- ♥ Get Into a Daily Rhythm and Routine

If you're a homeschooler, you've probably already noticed that sometimes people think we're nuts—

"How can you take on another full-time job when life is already busy enough?! "How do you work, run the house, make healthy meals, take time for yourself, and homeschool your kids?" "How do you organize your time and get everything done that you want to do without going crazy?"

In this chapter, you will learn a time management plan for creating your ideal yearly, monthly and daily schedules. You'll learn how to make schedules your tool, not your taskmaster. Scheduling every day isn't imperative. In fact, at times it can be counterproductive. Let your family find a daily rhythm in which you can function efficiently together. The most important part of this book is the goal-setting section. Everything builds from there. Scheduling your week, and if necessary your day, will help you reach your goals without feeling overwhelmed.

> **When I surveyed homeschoolers and asked them what
> their #1 challenge was, the most common response was,
> "Finding enough time to do it all!"**

This is why people think we are insane when we say we are going to homeschool our children instead of sending them to school for what is often six hours of free babysitting each day. But let's talk a minute about schedules. Some homeschoolers love schedules and some hate them. Some homeschoolers like to type out daily assignment sheets for each of their children. Some like to work on a rotation schedule, and each child has a special time when they get to work with the parent. Some homeschoolers like to have each of their children working in a separate room in the house so that they don't disturb each other. You decide what will work best for you. It is truly freeing to have balance and order in your life. Since you are a homeschooler and don't have a predictable public school schedule given to you in September, you get to create one for yourself.

♥ The Easy 4-Step Time Management Plan for Homeschoolers

Within the structure you create, you and your children will have the luxury to really focus on the tasks at hand. It can make studying more efficient. The great part is, organizing your school schedule is basically the same process as organizing your school supplies. In 4 easy steps, you are going to:

1) Identify time wasters so that you can eliminate these and instead schedule that time for yourself.
2) Decide what you want your homeschooling YEAR to look like.
3) Decide what you want your homeschooling WEEK to look like.
4) Create your DAILY homeschooling schedule or "rhythm."

Here's how one homeschooler describes how scheduling works for her family:

"We set goals for the year, then break those goals down into baby steps. Having a routine helps us to stay focused and on task, but we allow flexibility in terms of methods and even what we study. The children are involved in the planning process, so they get to help choose. We keep the mornings for their seatwork, and the afternoons for learning on their own, playing, exploring, reading, and other activities."

♥ Eliminate Time Clutter

In this system, you work backward from the big picture of how you typically spend your time. First, increase your available time by decreasing unnecessary activities by either a) delegating them to someone else; or b) eliminating them altogether. This will be like taking a "Before" and "After" picture. You can decide how much of it you want to do with your children.

Start by getting the "Before" picture—how you are currently spending your time:

- ✓ Write down a list of every little thing you do throughout the day and week.

- ✓ Rank them in decreasing order of priority and importance (see example).

- ✓ Decide which activities you can either eliminate or delegate.

- ✓ Take the amount of time you used to spend on unnecessary activities, and replace these with things that will recharge and replenish your energy. Taking care of ourselves as parents and teachers is absolutely imperative, yet these activities often get dropped or overlooked for too long. It is not selfish to take care of yourself. When you are in an airplane and the oxygen masks come down, you are instructed to put your own mask on first, before your child's. That's because you have to take care of yourself in order to take care of others.

Remember to take care of you. How are you going to take care of yourself so that you are always at your best? What are you going to do each day and each week so that you can recharge and refresh?

As you'll see in my sample activity list, I take time each morning to meditate, read, and enjoy a quiet cup of tea. I ranked those activities as a "1"—absolutely necessary and cannot be delegated. I also try to make sure that I exercise for at least an hour each day. Last, I try to get in bed early enough to watch a movie or read for awhile. This is how I relax.

For example, here is a working list of some of my activities. I ranked mine like this:

1 = absolutely necessary/cannot be delegated
2 = somewhat important/could possibly be delegated
3 = not very important/could definitely be delegated and may even be eliminated
4 = kind of a time waster/should probably be eliminated

Activity	Rank	Delegate?
Morning meditation, tea, & reading	1	no
Special date w/C before she goes to school	1	no
Making breakfast	2	yes
Making lunch	3	yes
Special weekly dinner	1	yes
Cooking lessons with kids	1	no
Other dinners	2	yes
Daily work on my business	2	no
Daily work on my goals	1	no
Daily exercise	1	no
Pleasure reading or movie in PM	3	no
Kids' doctor/dentist appointments	2	yes
Driving kids to classes/lessons	2	yes
Doing dishes	2	yes
Making beds	3	yes
Cleaning bathrooms	3	yes
Cleaning floors	3	yes
Daily tidy up	2/3	yes
Helping kids with their #1 goal	1	no
General homeschooling	2	some
Laundry	3	yes
Taking care of pets	2/3	yes
Field-trip Friday	3	maybe
Visiting Aunt on Sundays	1	no
Getting kids together w/friends	3	yes
Reading aloud in evening	2	no
Checking e-mail every 3 seconds	4	maybe
Taking calls during homeschooling time	4	machine
Playing Ping-Pong with family	2	no
Driving C to/from school	3	yes

Looking at this Activity Time Log, I don't have a lot of items I ranked as 4. This means that either I'm better organized than I think, or I was in denial when I wrote this list. I had a hard time identifying activities that are a 4. I suspect that it's because I should have listed more activities that are insidious time wasters, but I don't even realize I am doing them.

Now I'm going to add to this list and see if there is anything I do on a regular basis that is really just "time clutter," taking up unnecessary space in my schedule and I which I would be better off to let go. It's like saving money—find these activities and suddenly you'll have extra time to spend on something else you'd rather do.

If analyzing and organizing your time seems too regimented, relax. We all know that in a perfect world, nothing would interfere with our well-laid plans, but at some point in homeschooling, life will intervene, diverting your time, attention, resources or all of the above. If you started homeschooling on the typical school calendar (late August/early September), Month 4 brings the bustle of holiday activity. If you began during another month, consider yourself lucky if nothing pressing occurs within four months!

If you try to continue your typical homeschooling schedule and deal with the holiday (or other) bustle, you'll feel your candle is burning at both ends. Better instead to attend to life matters while taking advantage of homeschooling's flexibility. Allow your homeschooling to bend and twist to fit into life where it can. Get creative and turn the interruption—whether festive or not-so-festive—into a learning experience.

If the interruption requires a lot of time in the car, check out an armful of your library's books on tape. If the interruption involves spending time in a hospital or other waiting rooms, have your child bring along some good books, pen and paper, Mad Libs word games, and mystery, puzzle or brainteaser books. If the interruption involves getting the house ready for the holidays, consider it a month long arts-and-crafts period of decorating, cooking, baking and making gifts. Remember, life is learning, and your child's mind and heart will benefit from being included in "the stuff of life."

TIPS

♥ You don't need to give up homeschooling if a situation temporarily takes your attention away from it.

♥ From the arrival of a new child to the death of a loved one, homeschooling families find that sharing "the stuff of life" brings them closer and provides lessons that books can't provide.

♥ If appropriate, have your child or children take charge of the homeschooling. They just might surprise you with their abilities!

♥ Shape Your Yearly Calendar

Just like school, homeschooling seems to have times when a lot is getting done and others when practically nothing is getting done. Remember when you were in school? Pretty much nothing but art was done in December during the holidays. And in June, nothing much got accomplished because everyone was burned out and distracted with thoughts of the coming summer vacation.

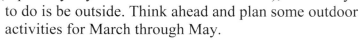
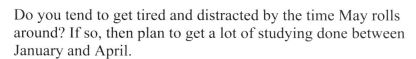

The beauty of homeschooling is its flexibility. YOU get to create a yearly schedule that works for you, along with and a daily schedule that works well for you and your kids.

Let's take a look at how your family tends to spend the year. Do you tend to get a lot done between September and November? If you do, then set some challenging goals for that part of the year, and perhaps decide ahead of time that if you reach your goals, you will take December off. Give the kids a vacation when it's a natural down time for them. Spring can be distracting (especially if you live in a cold winter area), when all you want to do is be outside. Think ahead and plan some outdoor activities for March through May.

Do you tend to get tired and distracted by the time May rolls around? If so, then plan to get a lot of studying done between January and April.

When my children were younger, we homeschooled year round. It was such a natural part of our day that no one wanted to stop. For my family, because I knew we were going year round, I felt comfortable scheduling days off during the week throughout the whole year, where no "official" homeschooling was planned. Now that my children are older, they seem to need that big break in the summer. They take a lot of group classes, and they are tired and burned out by the end of May.

Get out your calendar and think about what type of schedule will work best for you. Will you follow the typical school schedule, or will you school year round? No matter what you do, be sure to schedule plenty of breaks throughout the year to rest and recharge. Ask your children what they would like to do. This is what my family's homeschooling calendar looked like one year.

♥ August 15: First Day of Homeschool

The kids wanted to start their "official" homeschooling on August 15, which is the date their sister started high school. They wanted to go shopping for school supplies before then, and my youngest wanted to buy a back-to-school outfit for the first day. They love the idea of having their own art box, so we got that ready by the first day too. (This plan let us shop for school supplies when everyone else was, so we could take advantage of back-to-school sales.)

♥ December 1 through 31: Vacation

The kids wanted to take December off, and we agreed they could if they completed all their goals by then. I didn't know if my oldest homeschooler would be able to do this, because I didn't know his group and online class schedule yet. But we would try to make this happen.

♥ April: Spring Break

The kids decided that they would like to take a two-week trip in April, during Easter break. When we made the schedule, we voted on where to go.

♥ Mid-May: End of Schoolwork for the Year

They wanted to have all of their homeschooling done by the middle of May. My son would have the AP exams and the SAT II exams in May, so this plan made sense.

♥ Summer: Project Time

For the summer, the kids planned to relax, sleep in, and participate in an exciting summer program. For example, my 16-year-old son wanted to be an exchange student to either France or Belgium for a month. My 13-year-old daughter wanted to go to a dance camp, and my 11-year-old suggested she might want to go to a cooking camp.

The comfort of knowing what the yearly schedule will look like it that it eliminates the feeling of "Will this ever end?" By dividing your year into sections and setting goals for each time period, you get the satisfaction of checking things off your list and feeling like you have really accomplished something. And the kids get to celebrate and feel good about what they are doing.

SUGGESTION BOX

Here is how some other homeschoolers arrange their yearly schedule. Think about how these ideas might suit your own family's natural rhythms and activities.

"Pacing is important. We take a shorter summer vacation so that we can take a couple of weeks off in the spring, in the fall, and through all of December. It seems that the two most difficult times of the year are around the holidays when people are very busy, and spring, when the weather begins to turn. By scheduling breaks during these times we come back refreshed and ready to continue."

"Try to break up the school year into sections. Then when you complete a quarter, you can mark it off as completed! I feel like I have accomplished some big task, and the kids do too. Then you can reward the kids with a treat, like an ice cream at the ice cream parlor. Some places even give free ice cream, a kid's meal, or a pizza for good report cards. For an older child, maybe buy a new piece of clothing or jewelry --something inexpensive, though."

"I don't choose to do 'school at home' and I feel that helps us stay motivated because our learning is so much fun and so much a part of our lives. We do not stop living and take three hours and do 'school.' We learn all day long in our chores, our reading, our shopping, our playing, and our living."

"We have our long-term goal and then we break it down into smaller goals that we can see and finish easily. We also schedule more 'school days' than necessary so that we can take a mental health day when we need or want to."

"We take at least one day a month to go over what we did, what we need to learn, and what we want to see, do, or make (project). When we decide together, it gets the kids excited for what is to come -- even if we don't get to finish everything we had planned."

"An ounce of prevention is worth a pound of cure! We school the cores for 6 weeks on and then get one week off. We take off the cores from Thanksgiving to New Year's, also. During our breaks we still read, write, and have special field trips every day. External rewards get worked in every session or every other -- if we get our work finished in time all week, we can have a special game or movie night on Friday (or whatever the kids want)."

"Our family stays motivated by finding fun things to do all year round. If we are studying a certain subject we may do lap books, fieldtrips, movies, or some other activity related to that subject. We also find books to read that relate to what we are studying. Having a special-event day helps too, like bike day or picnic day or roller skating day."

How other homeschoolers design their ideal week...

"I complete weekly assignment sheets for those in high school. For my upper elementary students, I make daily assignment sheets and then work with them as needed. I then fit in the early elementary kids in the time frames that the 'olders' are working independently. For preschoolers, I keep them close by, working on things they enjoy. I have found that a great supply of stickers from the educational supply store is well worth the cost for keeping little hands occupied."

"We follow a very loose schedule. We do a subject a week, so we will do math one week, then history, then science, then language arts. There are certain things they do every day, like writing in a journal, free reading, art projects, and other projects that they have chosen to do."

"Each week I look at my calendar and mesh together my curriculum goals with my kids' outside activities, and then I plan my meals around those two things. Surprises still happen occasionally but at least most of the week will run smoothly."

"Every Friday is Nature/Exploring Day. We get outside and do hands-on science."

♥ Design Your Family's Ideal Week

Now that you have a general idea what your YEAR is going to look like, what is your WEEK going to look like? For example, last year, our family had Family Game Night every Tuesday night and we really enjoyed that. But they're bored with this now so we're trying to come up with a different theme for our family night this year. Maybe we'll have family pizza night on Fridays, or go out to eat once a week. Or maybe we just need new games.

Will you have a special theme for each day? For example, Monday is bike day, Tuesday is library day, Wednesday is art day, Thursday is homeschool park day, and Friday is backyard picnic day? Or perhaps you'll designate every Friday as "Field-trip Friday."

What type of weekly schedule will give your children variety and break things up a bit? You want to keep things from becoming too much the same, day after day. That's boring for everyone.

The keys to staying motivated are

1) Feeling like you are accomplishing something,
2) Celebrating along the way, and
3) Building flexibility into your yearly, your semester, and your daily schedule.

This is what my family's weekly schedule looks like (these are the activities that keep us motivated):

- Tuesday night is our family night.
- Friday is our volunteer day.
- On either Friday or Saturday night, I try to take a date with my husband.
- On Sundays I visit my elderly aunt.

♥ Find Your Perfect Daily Rhythm

Here is a bit of good news for anyone considering homeschooling.

Isn't it interesting that...

**On average, to do the same amount of studying
as a classroom student does in 6 to 8 hours,
high school age homeschoolers
need to work only about 4 hours a day.
Younger students need only 1 hour a day.**

A lot of classroom time is lost to "busy-work" and classroom management issues. So if the idea of homeschooling ever seems impossible, keep this in mind—homeschool time usually requires only one to four hours a day, depending on the age of the child. By spending some time up front designing your perfect curriculum and scheduling semester goals, you can make sure everything else falls into place around that core study time.

Okay, let's put it all together and decide what your daily schedule is going to be like. For example, this is what our daily schedule looked in 2008:

1) During my quiet time in the morning, I look at my day-timer to see what activities we have scheduled, and then I let the day flow around that. I make sure to schedule time for those things that I have said are my daily must-dos (like exercise, etc).

2) My 16-year-old's schedule is pretty much set in stone, since he has scheduled classes and tutoring times. I wake him up around 8:00 (at his request) and then work with him to follow his teacher's schedules and turn his work in on time. He knows from experience that if he studies four hours a day, he can keep up with his studies and feel on top of things. After he has done his four hours, he can watch movies or play computer games, guilt free!

3) For my 11-year-old daughter's schedule, I let her sleep in. While she's sleeping, I enjoy my quiet time, and then work in my home office until she wakes up. After breakfast she likes to do her writing and reading and math on her own by the fireplace, with a movie running in the background (this is how she says she works best). I come up from the office from 12:00 to 2:00 so that we can do studies together. I ask her, "What do you want to work on together today?"

Now it's your turn.

What will your daily schedule look like? How does everyone like their day to flow? Some children may be more focused early in the morning and be in the mood for intensive studying early in the day. Some children never quite wake up until noon and get into their rhythm later in the day. For others, it's easier to really concentrate after the sun's gone down.

How do you want your day to flow? Remember, you're not locked into an hour-by-hour schedule. Instead, you decide ahead of time what the basic structure of your day will be. This will help you live according to your priorities and focus your time and attention on the things that really matter to you.

Ideally, you can be flexible within your weekly schedule to accommodate for other factors like seasonal daylight savings time, sleep patterns, mealtimes, etc. For instance, you could keep one rhythm for a couple of months during the fall semester, then switch over to a different rhythm for the winter months when you may decide you and your kids want to sleep in until the house warms up. For our family, we often enjoy reading aloud for hours together at night in front of the fire.

After that, you may want to have a different rhythm planned for when the weather improves and you want to spend lots of time outdoors. By anticipating the holidays and the weather changes, you can decide ahead of time how much and what type of homeschooling you are planning to do during each time period. That way, you've planned ahead that you are going to spend lots of time on Christmas projects during December, lots of time for snow sports in January, and lots of time for biking in the spring.

What will your day look like? Will your rhythm be that everyone has to have their clothes on and hair brushed and teeth clean before breakfast? Then, studies between breakfast and lunch? Chores after lunch? Free time once the studies and chores are done? What will work best for your family? Will each child have his or her own study and chore list to work on each day at his or her own pace? For example, maybe you expect each child to read for 30 minutes and write in a journal every day, but it doesn't matter when these tasks are accomplished. Will you do studies together for an hour, break to unload the dishwasher and switch the laundry, do some more studies, and then break for another chore?

Are there certain things that you want to be sure you do every day? For example, no matter how tired I am, I want to be sure to visit with my older daughter every morning before she goes to school. And no matter how busy I am, I want to make sure that I take time to exercise each day. When my children were young, I made sure that no matter what was going on, I would read aloud to them for an hour or more each night. (I have the sweetest memories of those times.)

You don't need to pick a million things here, just one or two things that are top priority. And of course, now that you've read the chapter on goal-setting, one of the things on your list should, of course, be that you will take an action step daily toward your personal goal.

MORE FROM THE......... SUGGESTION BOX

Here are some examples of how other homeschoolers organize their day. Use these as inspiration, but remember that there is no one right way. The right way is the way that works best for you and your family.

"I use planners and try to fill them in two to three weeks ahead so that the kids can go on their own if they want."

"I do lessons with my daughter in the mornings and my son in the afternoon. Some history and science we do together, and they are evaluated at their own levels."

"Prayer first and foremost. I changed how we did schoolwork from time to time. Sometimes we would do school in our classroom at home, in the car while driving to our vacation spot, on the trampoline with Popsicle in hand, on the lawn with their pile of books, or at the river nearby (weather permitting). I normally set a schedule for school beginning at 9:00 AM and ending around 2:00 PM, with lunch and a break in between those hours."

"I spent many hours a day reading to both of our children. If we weren't reading together, we were making crafts and learning how things are put together. We discovered that for our children, learning was not a job, it was as exciting opportunity that they chose. Our children have a hand in picking out what they are interested in. We go through the different discipline areas and show them what we've found and then they choose."

"Our mornings are very structured, with 15- to 30-minute blocks of time to complete morning chores and seatwork for school. I have six children between the ages of 3 and 13, and this enables me to make sure that I spend time with each child individually. I do work full-time, as I run a business from home, and I have to be away from home occasionally. We work together as a family and plan our curriculum and activities around our family purpose and priorities."

"Because I have to work outside the home, our homeschool is very structured. I do the bulk of the schooling in the morning before I go to work, and then my husband takes over in the afternoon with reading and seatwork. Also, because my husband is retired, he takes on the cleaning of the home, and the kids all help by keeping their rooms clean."

"I use a daily schedule or agenda. During the heart of the school year, when all outside activities are in full swing, I schedule our day in 30-minute increments. The schedule isn't set in stone, but does guide us through the day. I make doctor appointments and other errands for times when we will be out for a scheduled activity. That minimizes the time it takes to get out of the house and the time it takes to settle back in once we get home. Having a printed schedule for daily and weekly chores is vital to making sure everything gets done at some point during the week. I have set times scheduled throughout the day (after breakfast, before lunch, and after school is done for the day) to pick up, do a few small chores and generally get the house in order. I get up about 1-1/2 to 2 hours before my children each day. This gives me an opportunity to have some quiet time, exercise, eat and shower before they arise for the day. Having a set wake-up time for everyone helps to get us off to a good start."

"I HAVE to have a routine. The laundry must be started before school begins, the kids have to have their chores done before they can have free time, and Fridays are house-cleaning days. School is mostly finished by lunchtime and afternoons are spent picking up and doing any extra schoolwork, then it's time to play until dinner. When Dad gets home, we're ready to eat and spend time with him. This routine keeps things relatively predictable throughout the week."

Balancing Laundry and Lessons....Literally!

Remember that homeschooling is like adding another part-time job onto what you are already doing. It's important to be gentle and kind with yourself. Appreciate all that you do, find an organization method that works for you, and make sure that you schedule in time for yourself. As they say, "If mom or dad isn't happy, then no one is happy." Homeschoolers find so many creative ways to combine their household chores with learning. Sometimes they are so seamlessly incorporated, kids find themselves learning math, while they're counting socks!

♥ Be Kind to Yourself!

Our children are with us for such a short time. In the long run, will it matter that the house is less than perfect? Everyone has a personal tolerance for messes and chaos. Honor your own level of tolerance. If you work best in a structured, tidy environment, then set up a schedule that works for you. If you work best with more freedom and flexibility, that's okay too. The key is not to try to be someone you're not, or to try to live up to someone else's expectations or standards. Set up a routine that works for you. Do you want to get all your studies done Monday through Thursday and then end the week with Field-trip Friday? Want to set up a daily or weekly chore and cooking schedule? Tell your children, "We need you. We can't possibly work, homeschool you and run the house without your help. We all have to pitch in."

SUGGESTION BOX

Here's what other Homeschoolers Say About How They Balance Work, Chores and Homeschooling...

"My office and schoolroom are in the same room. I often get my children started on independent schoolwork, and then do my own work. I will also leave the room for short periods. For example, I'll clean the bathroom for 15 minutes while my son finishes his math."

"Sometimes housework will suffer. You sometimes have to let that happen, because your child's education is far more important than dusting the house."

"I have found that once I came to terms with the fact that it's okay if you homeschool in the afternoons or the weekends, my life was MUCH easier. When I tried to stick to a traditional schedule my life was SO disorganized."

"We turn chores into schooling events. With the little ones this is simple, because we sort the laundry by color and size, count the pieces of clothes, etc... Everything we do we try to make a learning experience, so we can cover several subjects per day. The joy of homeschooling is not doing things in the traditional manner, and the kids just love it."

"I try to make it a family affair as well, for example, we say, let's break for a dishwasher load, or let's fold clothes while we discuss this project. And, of course, when things are done early, I reward them with a field trip or movie, something fun. They enjoy museums and field trips and do not realize I am teaching them, say, at the zoo. Everything can be explained in a way that ties in the school learning. My kids have scored in the upper 90th percentile for years!"

"I get up really early in the morning and try to have a routine for my chores. I get most of my housekeeping ideas from www.flylady.net. By doing a little bit of cleaning every day, I rarely have to do a big cleanup job. Also, I don't obsess over having a clean house, because that's just one of the sacrifices one makes when committing to keeping the children at home. I plan supper in the morning so that I am not in a hurry to get dinner on the table when my husband gets home, and we can all sit down and eat as soon as we are finished with our evening activities."

"Get help! Who said you have to do it all. Hire a housekeeper or a mother's helper to help with the chores and cooking, join a babysitting co-op, trade cooking for tutoring. Think of what you are not spending on private school tuition. And lower your standards. Who said you have to have everything perfect?"

"Chores (taking care of the animals we have) are always first, even before we ourselves eat. Cleaning chores are done after school and before any special activities. When grading is needed that day, I recruit the older child to help grade her younger siblings' work, and it gives her a feeling of great importance in the classroom."

"Our children feel like they are needed in the family. The chores they do prove to them that I need them to help make the household run smoothly. When they don't do their chores, the rest of the family suffers. School does not begin until chores are completed"

"Chores are done every night at 6:00 PM, after dinner, so when we get up, the house is clean. With six kids, they all have a chore and when they complete their chore they may have an hour of TV or playtime. They take outside time 90% of the time."

"We do not pay our children for chores. If chores are done, especially without being asked, there are rewards, but usually not money! I think this idea helps the girls have a sense of responsibility for their 'world.' Not only do they have the privilege of being home, but they are learning how to function as a team. There is no separation in my mind between chores and homeschooling. It all goes together!"

"We want our children to have good money skills, so we pay them for some of their chores. For example, my son's job is to unload the dishwasher and take care of the recycling, and he earns $5 a week for this. My youngest is in charge of taking care of all the pets, and my middle daughter is in charge of cleaning up the TV room every night before she goes to bed. When they want to buy something, we ask them, "Is this something you want to spend your money on?""

"In my house we call it the 'dash and stash.' I set the oven timer for 30 minutes, and we all run around the house putting things back in order. I explain to the kids that this is the power of synergy. When five of us work together for just 30 minutes, we get 2 ½ hours of cleaning done."

The Easy 3-Step Scheduler

For this assignment, now is to write down and rank all of your activities from 1 to 4 and then "dump the 4s." Ask your kids for their feedback. Can you also dump or delegate some of your 3s? Rate each activity as a 1 (very important to you), down to the unnecessary 4s (not important). Note whether or not this task can be delegated to another person, such as to your spouse, a child, or hired help.

Step 1 – Figure out how you spend your time, down to the minute.

It may seem silly, but you'd be surprised how the minutes can add up when you're spending 5 to 15 minutes here and there throughout the day on the phone, in front of the mirror or the TV, opening mail, or responding to emails. Be brutally honest with yourself.

Ask your spouse and kids to chime in and add to the list too. It'll be good for them to see you evaluating your schedule according to your goals. This will be a good skill for them to have too, and once again you are being a good role model on how to handle stress and live your life "on purpose."

Q: Write down everything you do in a day and rate these between 1 and 4. Are there any activities that you can drop?

A:_____
_____
_____

Q: Which activities can you delegate to someone else? Who can help you?

A:_____
_____
_____

Q: What are you going to add to your daily, weekly and yearly schedules in order to take care of yourself? What type of time and monetary investment are you willing to make in order to ensure that you stay at your best?

A:_____
_____
_____

Q: Who is going to help you with the cooking, cleaning, laundry, etc.? If your children help, then how are their chores going to be organized?

A:_____

_____

_____

Q: How are you going to track how your children are doing towards their goals? How are you going to celebrate?

A:_____

_____

_____

Step 2 – Factor your children's preferences into your daily and weekly schedules. Ask your children these questions:

Q: When do you learn best? What time of day?

A:_____

_____

_____

_____

Q: Do you have any suggestions on how we should organize our day?

A:_____

_____

_____

Q: What do you want your daily schedule to be like?

A:_____

_____

_____

Step 3 – Summarize your homeschooling schedule.

Describe your homeschooling schedule in 50 words or less. This way you're taking something that is potentially big and scary and complicated and proving to yourself that it is really quite simple. Here is my summary:

"My son will study for four hours a day, after which he can watch movies and play his computer games. And I will homeschool with my daughter M-F from 12:00 to 2:00, having fun and working from her goal list." (40 words)

You can do it. Write *YOUR* 50-word summary of your homeschooling schedule.

A:_____
_____
_____
_____
_____
_____
_____

Q: What will your year look like? Write down what your goals are, schedule-wise, for the YEAR. Fill in your homeschooling calendar.

A:_____
_____
_____
_____
_____
_____

Q: What will your week look like? Write down what your goals are, schedule-wise, for the WEEK. Then fill in your weekly schedule and post it in your family's work space.

A:_____
_____
_____
_____
_____
_____

Q: What do you really want to make sure that you do every day? Write down what your goals are, schedule-wise, for your DAY.

A:_____
_____
_____
_____
_____
_____

CHAPTER EIGHT

GET YOUR TEENS INTO THEIR FIRST-CHOICE COLLEGE

- ♥ **Research College Requirements**
- ♥ **Graduate High School with Flying Colors**
- ♥ **Develop the Curriculum That Will Qualify Your Children for Their First-Choice College**
- ♥ **Go for It!**

Homeschoolers and parents of public school students alike worry about whether their children will be accepted to top-notch colleges and universities. Because homeschoolers have expressed so many concerns about how to prepare their children for higher education, I interviewed some of the top admissions experts in the country. After speaking with the admissions directors of Harvard University, Purdue University, and the University of Texas – all of them homeschooler-friendly – this is what I discovered...

♥ What Colleges Are Looking For

According to Harvard's Director of Admissions, Marylyn McGrath Lewis, Harvard University uses the same requirements for homeschoolers and traditional students:

There is no single academic path we expect all students to follow, but the strongest applicants follow the most rigorous secondary school curricula available to them. An ideal four-year preparatory program includes four years of English, with extensive practice in writing; four years of math; four years of science: biology, chemistry, physics, and an advanced course in one of these subjects; three years of history, including American and European history; and four years of one foreign language. In addition to academic standing, Harvard is looking for well-rounded individuals who have participated in personal development outside the institution...Follow the passions you have and develop them. We are looking for nonacademic criteria – maturity, social facility, and nonacademic talents, which is the same range as for traditional students.

Harvard requires applicants to submit the results of either the SAT I or ACT standardized test, and the results of three SAT II Subject Tests to demonstrate a mixture of academic interests.

According to Jo Anne Brown, Senior Associate Director at the Office of Admissions at Purdue:

I would give homeschoolers the same advice as other applicants...Be involved in outside activities, either in the community or in connection with a school. Have strong academic credentials and take the SAT or ACT twice, first in the spring of junior year and again in the fall of your senior year. Purdue uses the better score on the tests, whatever helps the applicant the most... Apply early and visit the campus. Use our website to get as much information as possible about the university, and make contact with somebody at the institution.

Kedra Ishop, Associate Director of Admissions at the University of Texas, says:

To help us make a decision about your admission, the Office of Admissions will review your file, looking for evidence that you excelled both academically and personally. That's why it's critical for you to include as much information about what and how you studied, how you enhanced your learning experiences, and the activities that you participated in during your high school years. Reviewing the list of factors we consider for all applicants may help you to determine what relevant information to include as part of your application.

120

♥ College Requirements at a Glance

Basic requirements for admission vary by institution, but these are the common requests:
- A high school diploma, a parent's transcript, or GED
- Class rank
- SAT or ACT and SAT II test scores
- Resume or portfolio review (which can include works of art, acting or music tapes, or video game or software design)
- Written essays
- Interviews and/or entrance examinations

In addition, most colleges expect your child to have:

- Four years of English, math, history, science, and a foreign language
- High scores on the SAT and/or ACT exams; (passing scores on Advanced Placement (AP) exams are a bonus
- 200 hours of volunteer service throughout high school
- A resume of extracurricular activities and interests

Your best approach is to check with the admissions office to determine the specific requirements of any schools in which you are interested.

**Be sure any college to which you want
to apply does accept homeschoolers.
The good news is that almost all do.**

♥ Prepare Your Children for the Life They Want

Although it's important to know what is required for college admission, remember that we are really preparing our children to be able to do what *they* want to do with their lives, not what colleges want them to do. And of course, we want the best for our children. It's easy to get caught up in trying to meet college admission requirements. However, just because your teens want to go to a particular institution of higher learning doesn't mean they should compromise their goals and dreams to get there.

When my oldest was 16 and we were knee-deep in the whole college admissions process, I nearly made a big mistake with his homeschooling. When my children were young, my top priority was to keep our homeschooling fun and enjoyable. Then, when my son became a ninth-grader, I got scared. I suddenly took on a "nose to the grindstone" approach to education and forgot all about our emphasis on what he wanted, because I was worried. Why? I was worried that if my son didn't do his studies exactly by the book, and if he didn't work twice as hard as he always had, he would never be able to get into a good college – and then I would have failed him. I wrote up a very strict learning plan for him that went totally by the book (or what I imagined the "book" to be). It was rigorous, unimaginative, and restrictive, and it did not reflect my son's interests or talents at all!

Then it dawned on me…What kind of life was I preparing him for? Was this where the enslavement begins? First I told him he can do whatever he wants, then I asked him to live a "have to" existence for high school so that he could get into college. He would go to college because "you have to get a good job." Then he would endure year after year of a "have to" job in order to be a good provider. Where would it stop? Would he wake up one morning in his thirties or forties and think, "Is this all there is to life?"

I want my children to live a "want-to" life, not a "have-to" existence. Henry David Thoreau once said, "The mass of men lead lives of quiet desperation." Now, that's a scary thought! I don't want that for myself, my husband, or my children. I'm convinced there is a better way. So, whether your child wants to go to college or explore non-college alternatives, first, keep in mind why you homeschool in the first place.

♥ Set Your Teens' Curriculum to Suit Their Future

There are ways to fulfill college requirements and life dreams to create win-win outcomes. With my son, we decided to prepare him for college and for life by taking his interests and goals to heart and building his curriculum around these. My son wanted to write a book, and he wanted to design video games, so we made these goals our top priorities for his junior year. And I'm convinced that colleges will be impressed by this. If he has a published book in his hands and a portfolio of games he has created, he will definitely stand out in the admissions process, don't you think? And if a college isn't impressed by these things, then that college is not the college for him, as far as we are concerned. Otherwise, what is the point, if not to live life on one's own terms?

For his junior year, then, we did not plan to do science, even though "the book" says that colleges want four years of science. He would work on writing his novel instead, because that was important to him. This is what he is best and this is where he really shines.

While I was in my scared mode, I was also looking for any Advanced Placement classes I could get my hands on, whether he liked the subject or not. For example, I really wanted him to take AP English Literature because I thought the class would be interesting and the writing skills useful for his future. And it was. AP Lit was totally worth his time. But I almost signed him up for AP Psychology too, even though my son has no interest in this subject. Then I caught myself again and thought, "Wait a minute. Can't I find him a great online AP class in a subject he really likes and would really enjoy?" And I found an AP European History class at www.Homeschool-Teachers.com that he was very excited about, since he loves learning about wars, and he wants to live in Europe. The choice was a win-win. Why would I over prepare him for a life he doesn't want to live and under-prepare him in the areas he wants to pursue?

My son also really wanted to be fluent in French, so I found an excellent tutor who would teach him French and help him prepare for the AP French exam. Another win-win situation. The AP exam scores would will look good on his college applications and they would be in subject areas that he interest him. Helen Keller once said that "Life is a daring adventure or nothing at all." Don't we want our children's lives to be an adventure too?

One Homeschool.com Product Tester wrote this advice:

The kids investigated their chosen career paths and then figured out what is required to become gainfully employed in that chosen field. If continuing education is required, they investigated the costs of the education and the requirements to get into the school of their choice.

Now that we've talked about the importance of honoring your teen's interests, let's go back to square one—creating a curriculum for your college-bound teens. We're also going to go over some great non-college alternatives in the next chapter. For now, however, I will assume that you want your teens to get their high school diploma, and you want them to prepare for college so that, if they should decide to go, they will have laid the groundwork to make that a feasible choice.

Remember how satisfying it was in the goal-setting chapter when you were asked to think about your goals and what you want in life? Perhaps no one had ever asked you that before. And remember how surprised and excited your children became when you asked them to list their goals? Well, now their time line is a little tighter, so your college-bound kids will set some very specific goals and the dates by which they will need to be completed.

♥ Graduation Requirements Made Easy

In many ways, homeschooling teenagers is different that teaching other age groups. It's also easier than you might think. It just takes a little more planning and organization. Depending on how advanced their studies are and what your own level of knowledge or expertise is, you may need to set aside a budget for tutors. Your teen's time line becomes much tighter as their last years progress and as state-scheduled tests and college

application submission deadlines approach. None of this has to translate into more pressure, however, if you think ahead. That's what we're going to do here—create a time line for your teens to prepare them for graduation, and if they want, get them into college. This doesn't have to mean more time. As I said in the last chapter, all of this, and more, can be done by homeschooling just four hours a day. Classroom students typically need 6- to 8 hours a day because a lot of time is lost to busywork and classroom management issues.

Isn't it interesting…

On average, high school homeschoolers can do excellent college-level work studying just four hours a day.

♥ Preparing Them For Their First-Choice College

You can begin the process of preparing your teen for college as early as possible, even as early as junior high school. Ask your children what careers they are interested in and then build their curriculum around that.

Here's a thought…
Look into having your child take as many junior college classes as possible while he or she is still in high school. This will give your child a taste of college, and possibly save on tuition later.

♥ Research Colleges
Talk to your children about their choices. Let this be part of the research process, and stay as open-minded as possible about their intentions. (For this, you'll want to have also read Chapter 9 "Non-College Alternatives" in case they have other ideas for how they want to spend their next few years after graduating from high school.) Think about your own experience. What are your and your spouse's attitudes about attending a university? Did you go to college? Do you want your children to go to college? If so, what are your reasons?

Look at the different colleges that he might want to attend. Find out their specific requirements and write them down. A thorough listing of colleges, descriptions, and college requirements can be found at www.Collegeboard.com. I suggested to my son that he may change his mind about being a video game designer, so it might be good to find colleges that offer other majors he would like too, such as business, entrepreneurship, and writing. And he says that he doesn't want to attend a really large college, so we will focus on smaller schools.

♥ Select the Colleges to Which Your Child Wants to Apply
After extensive college research, select with your child six to eight colleges that you think your child might like to attend -- two that are really hard to get into, four that he or she can probably get into, and two safety colleges. The choices are not set in stone at this point. A "stretch college" is a college that your child has a slim chance of getting into, but if he does, you'll be doing a major happy dance.

Financial Aid and Scholarships
If you are hesitant at all about a college just because of financial concerns, please don't be. My son and I plan to spend the summer after his junior year researching and applying for any and all scholarships we can get our hands on. When I was in high school I received a lot of scholarships, not because I was so smart, but because I bothered to apply.

A Word About Financial Aid And Scholarships.

As much as possible, please don't allow lack of funds to be the reason a child cannot apply to the colleges of their choice. There is so much money out there for anyone who wants to get a higher education. At this early stage, it would be a shame if your child eliminated possibilities.

♥ **Where There Is a Will, There Is Always a Way…**

…And I would add: Where there is desire, determination, and diligence, there is definitely a way.

Start your research a year before college entrance, but be thinking about it even earlier. If your child does really well in one subject and this is also his or her area of interest, see if he or she could get a scholarship in that area. There's no harm in checking private scholarships and finding out what types of achievements they target. Excelling in a favorite subject can literally pay off when it comes time for college.

In addition to the following websites, I also recommend the book *Great Colleges for B Students* by Tamra Orr. It is available from Amazon.com.

www.homeschool2college.com .
This site offers a binder-type book that walks you through all of the financial aid steps. The Weavers received over $125,000 in no-repay college financial support for their two daughters.

www.paylessforcollege.com
This site is by Reecy Arresty. He is a college admissions and financial aid expert.

www.Homeschool.com/Homeschool Contests And Scholorships/default.asp
Homeschoo.com offers a searchable database of contests and scholarships for all ages.

Here are some excellent college admissions tips from Reecy Arresty, the author of: *How to Pay for College Without Going Broke.*

1) Have your teen meet with the university Dean, Director of Admissions, and Head of Department for his/her first-choice college.

Show that person your resume, business card, and a letter stating:
"Why I Must Attend _____ University." Ask this person, "How can I improve upon what I am doing so that I can get accepted here?"

2) Make sure your child is up on current events so that he or she can converse intelligently during the interview.

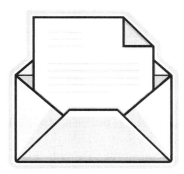

3) To prepare for the verbal section of the SAT, have your child use a dictionary to learn three new English words each week. To help with a foreign language, have your child learn three new words a week in that language.

4) Colleges expect applicants to have 200+ hours of volunteer work on their resume and they love it if your child starts his own volunteering or fund-raising campaign.

5) Letters of recommendation should never come from a parent. These are better coming from a teacher, volunteer organization, company executive, or other mentor.

6) A high school diploma is preferable to the GED. Find out what the diploma requirements are for your state and make sure you are on course to receive it. Simply Google the name of your state or Canadian province and then the words "diploma requirements."

7) Find out what homeschoolers do in your state regarding transcripts. Should you have your homeschool appear as a private school? Should you sign up with a curriculum provider or charter school? What would be the best option for your family?

♥   **Plan Your High School Curriculum Accordingly**

When planning your curriculum, remember to work backward from your career and college goals. Figure out how you can fulfill the requirements of your teen's first-choice College. Ask your teen, "What would you like to learn for history this semester? For science?"

As I mentioned, my oldest child wanted to become a video game designer so we worked that goal into his curriculum. For example, we found some excellent online classes through www.YDACS.com (the Youth Digital Arts Cyber School), and he has taken the classes "Video Game Design 101, 102 and 103." He also attended a four-week summer session of Game Design Academy at Stanford, offered by iD Tech Camps. (www.InternalDrive.com).

Most colleges expect applicants to have taken four years each of English, history, math, science and foreign language. For diploma requirements, you'll have to either do a Google search or ask a local homeschooler for the graduation requirements for your state. Remember to include your child's goals when working toward these requirements. For example, your child can choose what they want to learn for biology that year, and what type of experiments they want to do for chemistry that year. As parents, our primary goal for our children is to help them develop their special talents, and the way we do this is by helping them identify what interests them. Fortunately, homeschooling is so much faster than regular school that we have more time for "electives" and fun projects and programs. We want to keep asking our children every year, "What are your goals for this semester?" "What do you want to learn about?"

In the high school comments sent in by other homeschoolers, one piece of advice kept coming up over and over:

Your child can take dual enrollment classes at your local junior college and receive both high school and college credits for the same class.

For my son's senior year we planned to have him take some or all of his classes at our local junior college. There are several advantages to this.

♥ Advantages to Taking Local Junior College Classes

1) Most junior colleges allow dual enrollment, which means your child receives both high school and college credit for every class he takes. This looks impressive on college applications, and your teen can start college with college units already under his belt. This will save time and tuition when he enters a university full-time.

2) She will get experience on a college campus and can prove to herself and to prospective colleges that she can do well in a college environment.

3) He can take advantage of the college's resources, including science labs, art studios, libraries, and campus lecture series.

♥ Take All Required Tests and Other Recommended Tests

Know your high school testing schedule. Here is a listing of the possible tests your child may need to take.

High School Exit Exam
Does your state require an exit exam? If it does, then the exam is generally administered first in January of the sophomore year. Your teen can take it as many times as he needs to in order to pass it. Contact your local homeschooling group or public high school to see if you are required to pass an exit exam.

PSAT
The PSAT is administered in the fall of the sophomore or junior year. Colleges are notified of those students who do really well on this exam, so taking it can help with college admissions. A high score also can help with scholarships.

I called our local public high school and told them that my homeschooled son would be taking the PSAT, then asked if he could take it at the same time as their students. They were very accommodating.

Advanced Placement Exams
These exams are optional, but if your teen can pass three AP exams, then she is considered to be an AP Scholar. Colleges have no idea how in-depth your child's education has been, so high test scores provide outside verification that your child is a top student. AP exams are given only once a year, in May, and you sign up for them in early February. Perhaps you can find an online AP class in a subject area that your child is interested in.

The online AP English Literature class that my son took was just fabulous. (It was offered through www.homeschool-teachers.com.) The writing training alone was well worth the course, and my son's writing is now 200% better than it was before he took this class. This will help him with the SAT writing section too. Since your teen needs to take history and science classes anyway, why not take these as AP classes? And be sure to ask any potential AP teachers what their AP pass rate is. You want a teacher or tutor who can really prepare your child to pass the exam. See if you can take one AP class in the sophomore year, one in the junior year, and one in the senior year. My son took one AP class his sophomore year (AP Lit) and two AP classes his junior year (European History and French). If he passed all three exams, he could say that he is an AP Scholar when applying to colleges in his senior year. And if he didn't pass, he still would have taken excellent classes from topnotch teachers. Applications for the AP exam are at www.collegeboard.com or you can get them through your local public high school.

SAT/ACT and SAT II Exams

When I was a kid, we only had one shot to get a high SAT score. If you were having a bad day or had a case of nerves, that was just too bad. But now, kids take the SAT and ACT exams two or three times and colleges count your highest score. When you are researching colleges, find out if they prefer the SAT or ACT exam. Then plan accordingly.

Find out if they want applicants to take SAT II subject exams. Many universities want them to have taken three of these; usually one math and one English, and then either a history, science or foreign language exam. These exams are usually taken in May, at the end of the junior year. Your teen can sign up for these exams at www.collegeboard.com.

My son would be taking his first SAT in March of his junior year and then again two months later. That way he would have the highest test scores when he started applying to colleges in August or September of his senior year. We used a math tutor to help him prepare for the SAT to fill in any holes he might have in math, but we would just use SAT prep books to prepare him for the verbal section. We think his writing should be okay, since he worked so hard on it when he was preparing for the AP English Literature exam. He would also take three SAT II subject exams in May of his junior year.

Yes, we live in a test-crazy world, don't we?

♥   **Preparing College Applications**

Your teen should start applying for colleges and for financial aid in the fall of his or her senior year. Remember, you want your teen to apply to two colleges that are hard to get into, four that he or she will most likely be able to get into, and two safety colleges.

To narrow down the list of possibilities, visit as many of the campuses as you can. We planned to travel to see the colleges and try to talk with some students and faculty on the campus —this would help my son decide which colleges he would actually apply to. You can only learn so much about a college by reading about it. It's helpful to actually visit the campus so that you can get a real feel for it. For example, I know that my son didn't want to attend a college that is too large, and my daughter didn't want to attend a college that is too small. For myself, I knew the minute I visited my college thirty years ago, University of the Pacific, that it was the right place for me. On the other hand, you can wait and visit only those colleges that send an acceptance letter. The visit will help your teen decide which invitations he or she wants to accept and will prevent heartbreak if your teen falls in love with a place and then doesn't get in.

Gather your child's transcripts, credits, GPA, and other required documents for each application. If you homeschool with an outside umbrella organization, such as a church, a charter school, a curriculum provider, or an ISP (independent study provider), check with them to see if they can help prepare your child's high school transcripts. If you are going to prepare your own materials, here are some resources that can help:

www.HomeschoolOasis.com
This site, by Barb Shelton, has a lot of great resources for record keeping and organization.

www.homeschool2college.com by Linda & Joe Weaver.
The Weavers have forms to help you create transcripts and with other record keeping.

♥   **Graduate and Celebrate!**

We belong to a homeschool charter school in our area, and they take care of transcripts, diploma, graduation ceremony, prom, and other events that are popular in public schools. However, I still wanted to have a private graduation ceremony for my son at home – and I started planning the event two years ahead of time. High school graduation is such an important rite of passage in our society and I want my son's graduation to be just as special—and perhaps more personal—than his friends' and cousins' public school graduation ceremonies. Homeschoolers work incredibly hard and deserve this validation of all their efforts. Creating a special celebration and ceremony is a wonderful way to share their accomplishments with extended family and friends. Graduating marks not only the end of a whole era in your child's life, it is the initiation into a new world of responsibilities and dreams to come true!

SUGGESTION BOX

How Other Homeschoolers Have Prepared Their Teens for College...

"If your child even thinks he may want to attend college, then it's important to start early, 7th or 8th grade even, with discussions about the types of classes and tests colleges may want. My oldest son is 12 and we recently sat down and looked at college websites and compared their entrance requirements against our state's graduation requirements. Together we laid out the whole plan through graduation, including notes on which classes were a must and which were electives or suggested. He is free to change the plan down the road if his interests change, but at least he has a plan in place. We know which classes we'll do at home and which we'll want to outsource. We have an answer to 'But what about chemistry?'"

"Our homeschooled daughter just received a GREAT scholarship to Auburn University in Alabama. She will also be involved in their Honors Program. Her ACT score was 31. She applied to four state schools and received at least total tuition scholarships to each. She was highly sought after. No one ever questioned her homeschooling. Alabama is a great place to apply to college."

"I have a 20-year-old home school graduate who attends Greenville College in Greenville, Illinois. He is studying Digital Media, with an emphasis in sound engineering. Even though he had relatively low test scores, he was still able to get into the college of his choice."

"The best thing I did was buy an SAT CD and begin my 9th-graders on it. I mixed the questions into their current curriculum so that when it was time to study for the exam in their junior year, they were ready and understood how to answer the questions. It was not foreign or intimidating to them in any way. They were studying for years before they took the test formally."

"I am having my high-schooler take as many classes as we can handle, and she takes local community college classes that count as duel credit (high school credit and college credit). My advice is to take only those classes that are transferable to college or that help with a specialty that the student might need (i.e., medical terminology)."

"I feel right now the best skill I can equip them with is study skills and learning how to be an independent learner. My children have been taking notes since third grade. By high school I imagine notetaking will be a reflex."

"I am graduating a senior this Saturday. We had her take dual credit courses at our community college and she earned nine college credits this year. If I had been smarter, I would have enrolled her last year and done only dual credit classes instead of our homeschool classes. She could have had almost ALL of her core classes for college finished BEFORE she even graduated. I might add that she is not an above-average student, so it's something most kids can do."

"We are teaching our daughter how to study, take notes, and take tests. She is already taking college-level classes. We are helping her practice taking standardized tests while making sure not to put too much emphasis on them, as public schools do, and making sure to prepare her for real life as well"

"We do a lot of reading, online and offline. Join online homeschool groups and get inspiration from others who are currently handling high school. I keep track of useful information, suggestions, books, websites, etc. that they offer. We have a supervisor teacher and have access to a homeschool assistance program. We can ask questions or get advice from these sources when the time comes, -- which is approaching a lot faster than I'd like it to."

"I am looking over the requirements for high school graduation in our state. I will also contact some colleges to see what they will look for in a homeschool graduate. I use a software program to track assignments, grades and other activities. As we enter the high school years, I will be more specific in reporting what my student does in order to create viable transcripts when they are needed."

"When my oldest was entering high school, I sat down with him and asked him what he thought he needed in order to 'make it' once he graduated, and also which of his interests he wanted to pursue. We made a plan for his high school years and revised it every year."

"I teach the kids three things: 1) Have at least a rough draft of a book they are writing, 2) start a business or sign up under an existing one, and 3) work on math for the last two years."

"I have decided to use a company to make my transcripts for my high schooler. I teach what and how I want and send them the info, and they make transcripts for me. I feel it's worth the price; around $400 for two kids."

"My son knows what he wants to do, so that makes it easier. I'm following what our state requires for high school graduation, and am looking into what the colleges are looking for. I've found curriculum that fits those requirements and my son's learning style. We keep our eyes open for classes, seminars, etc. geared toward his subject. A local college offered exactly what he was looking for, just for high schoolers."

"I stress independent work, learning to 'dig it out' for themselves. I also have found that lots of writing projects are important to prepare for college-level work. It is not a particularly exciting text, but my daughter says that *Jensen's Format Writing* [by Frode Jensen] thoroughly prepared her for her university composition courses. She was a chemistry major and was hired her freshman year by the writing lab as a tutor. This was usually reserved for senior English majors."

"I am having my children begin taking ACTs in about 9th grade and continuing until they achieve their best score. I am beginning to check on how to enroll my daughter in dual classes at some point for her junior year. I am coordinating closely with my covering teacher. My daughter is also co-oping and helping to save for college. We are also trying to work in more essays to improve writing."

"My oldest daughter is preparing to 'test out of high school' -- that is, get her GED or state diploma -- at the end of this year. She'll only be sixteen, but she's ready for it. The program offers a full graduation ceremony with cap and gown. She's excited for that, and we'll have the dinner afterward."

My Plan for Getting Into My First-Choice College
(For parents and kids)

Begin with the end in mind; Start your high school and college planning by asking your teen these questions. Then plan your curriculum around his or her answers.

Q: Parents, what are your thoughts about college? Did you go to college? Do you want your children to go to college? If so, why? If not, why not?

A:_____

_____

_____

_____

Q: Ask your child, "What are you thinking about for a career? Do you have any ideas about what you'd like to be when you grow up? What are some things you will hope your job offers you (such as working conditions, hours, autonomy, ability for advancement)?"

A:_____

_____

_____

Q: Ask your child, "Have you thought about what you would like to major in at college? Since you want to become a _____, you may want to major in _____."

A:_____

_____

_____

Q: Ask your child, "Have you thought about which colleges you might want to attend?"

A:_____

_____

_____

Q: Colleges now expect you to have about 200+ hours of volunteering. My children have earned their volunteer hours in a number of ways; visiting retirement homes, taking care of exchange students, and fostering kittens. Children who are involved in the Scouts also tend to earn a lot of volunteer hours. Ask your teen, "Where would you enjoy volunteering" Then, be sure to keep track of the hours and get a letter of recommendation from the volunteer supervisor.

A:_____

_____

_____

Q: Explain to your teen: "If you think you might want to major in _____ and you think you would like to attend_____ college, then these are the courses you will need to take in high school."

A:_____

_____

_____

"And these are the test stores that you will need to attain on the SAT _____or ACT_____.

" So, let's plan your high school years and make sure we include lots of projects and activities that highlight and develop your special talents and interests."

Q: What are your teen's goals for this year?

A:_____

_____

_____

_____

_____

Q: Find out due dates for applications, test dates, etc. for each college. Put all these on your yearly calendar.

A: _____

_____

Q: Ask your teen, "How would you like to celebrate graduation?"

A:_____

_____

CHAPTER NINE

TO COLLEGE OR NOT TO COLLEGE?
That Is the Question

- ♥ **Know Your Options**
- ♥ **Choose Your Path**
- ♥ **Live the Life You've Dreamed Of**

"College may give you four years to park yourself, but the meter's running, make no mistake."

~ Danielle Wood, author of *The Uncollege Alternative*

Homeschooled children are usually at an advantage when it comes to knowing what they want to do after high school because they have had more time and opportunities to pursue different interests. If your teen is not interested in college and she does not have to support herself right away, you might want to give her room to explore her options. Whether her pursuits include a paycheck or not, the experience, new skills and confidence she acquires will pay off in spades. The world is her oyster now. Let her dig in.

♥ Life After High School

The only certainty these days is change – fast change. We're in the Information Age, and things change in the blink of an eye. Children today are not likely to have just one job that they keep for life. You are training your children to keep their eye on the ball, to identify what they want -- and how they can serve others -- knowing they can do anything they set their mind to.

What is next for your teen? What if they're not sure they want to go straight off to college? Maybe they're so involved in the community, they don't want to leave. Or maybe they're eager to see the world they've been learning about in books all these years. Maybe they just want to wait another year while they gain more real-world skills. Maybe they want to start a business and are ready to jump right in.

These are all good options. (Bill Gates is a big role model for youth these days, so don't be surprised if they argue that they don't need a college degree to be successful.) These days, there are plenty of very positive and productive alternatives to college…none of which indicates you have wasted your time. After all, you've been preparing your children for life…and here it is. Now what?

Start by congratulating yourself on a job well done. Congratulations!

You homeschooled your child all the way through high school. You nurtured the growth of a very special and unique individual, who is about to make his own contribution to society. You took on something very few people do and you did it well— educating a child. Perhaps you were afraid you couldn't do it at first, especially not alone, yet you were never alone. Together you and your child, probably with the support of a spouse, siblings and other homeschoolers, you did it!

Before you both launch into a full course in *Now What 101*, think about taking a break from planning. Maybe a family trip is called for. Or just some down time for both of you to relax and feel good about yourselves. Enjoy some time to do whatever you both want to do -- off the clock and not as part of any curriculum. Life will take off at 100 mph again soon enough. Treat yourself to a guilty pleasure such as reading a romance novel or magazine with no merit whatsoever and zero educational value. Maybe your teen wants to play video games or hang out with friends for a while. Indulge yourselves. Turn the off switch for the summer maybe or just a few days if you're someone who actually doesn't enjoy sitting on your laurels. When your batteries are recharged, you will automatically get excited about the opportunities that lie ahead. You can also set your internal clock to kick back into gear when it's time to put together that list of wonderful ideas for next year. Those ideas will likely keep popping into your head, inspiring you to move forward. Write these down on next year's goal list while they're still fresh in your mind. This goes for you and for your recent grad.

You know that the grand educational experiment is never over. Your child's interests will evolve, family circumstances will change, and experience will provide ever increasing wisdom about your child and yourself. Learning, you've discovered, is like breathing—it happens even when you're not conscious of it. Knowing this truth, your family now appreciates learning as part of a lifelong journey, instead of merely a means to an end. Acting as your child's guide on the adventure is the most rewarding job you'll ever have.

♥ How Do You Know You've Done a Good Job?

You may find yourself assessing your child's academic progress. It's likely you'll be evaluating your results and comparing them to others you've heard or read about, trying to figure out how you scored on the "socialization issue," and maybe still gauging if you've convinced your mother-in-law that homeschooling really is a great idea.

It's okay to use this time to assess the aspects of your learning lifestyle and where you are in terms of fulfilling your family's values, ideals and goals. Just don't get overly critical of yourself or your child. It is far more fruitful to ask yourself questions such as:
- ♥ Has your relationship with your child improved or grown stronger?
- ♥ Are family members happy and healthy?
- ♥ Is your child learning to be kind, honest, respectful, self-reliant and responsible?
- ♥ Has she learned how to think, express herself and enjoy increased self-esteem as a result?

If you can answer yes to all or most of these questions, you've done a good job. Still, don't be shy about evaluating your own experience and learning so that you can understand how to be happier, less stressed and more comfortable in your role as a learning guide. Because here's a tip you may not realize…your job doesn't stop here! A growing number of homeschoolers are beginning to ask the obvious question: If homeschooling works so well for elementary school and high school, can't it work well for college too? Can our children continue to give themselves a first-rate education without going to college?

There are good reasons and foolish reasons to go to college. If your child loves being in a classroom or knows she wants to become a doctor or a teacher, then college may be the right choice for her. On the other hand, every year thousands of kids go off to college because they don't know what else to do. This is understandable. It is the rare person who knows what they want to do the rest of their life when they are only eighteen years old.

**College can be an expensive place to figure out what you want to do.
Sometimes taking another year to figure that out is appropriate.**

My husband and I are homeschooling our children with the assumption that they will go to college -- not because we believe that college is the formula for instant success, but because we both went to college and loved it. In college there are so many different types of people and different nationalities and religions, all gathered together for a common purpose. I loved that part. And it was the only time in my life when I had a chance to mingle with soon-to-be lawyers, doctors, engineers, teachers, scientists, writers, you name it! I loved the diversity that college offered and want my kids to experience that. And for me, college was really fun. I was able to go to Japan for my sophomore year and Washington D.C. for my junior year. I would like my children to have these types of exciting experiences too. That being said, we are still leaving it up to our children to choose what they feel is best for them.

**As on any test, life is multiple choice.
The difference is, we often have the option to change our answers along the way.**

♥ Multiple Choice Options

If your child does not want to go to college, or is unsure, consider the following non-college alternatives:

♥ Internships and Apprenticeships

Internships and apprenticeships are a great way to get a taste of the adult world. Have your children test their resolve with some real hands-on work in the area of their interest. Volunteering can also fulfill a much deeper sense of purpose in a teen. It's a good way to see the contribution they can make for others.

Your child could be applying for internships at the same time he is applying for colleges. This is a good option if he is torn between majors. If he's undecided between one college that has a particularly good reputation in psychology, for example, and another that is more sciences-based, a six-month internship at a biology lab and another six months at a psych ward is going to make his preferences much clearer. In fact, the experiences will probably decide it for him. Then he can choose the college that is stronger in that area, and you have not spent two years' tuition for him to come to this same conclusion.

I have a friend who thought she wanted to be a psychologist, so she went to a school whose strong suit was psychology. Within the first year of volunteering on a crisis hotline, she realized this wasn't for her, and she wanted to be a writer instead. By then, she was already one year into a school with a very weak writing program. At this stage, it's never too late to reapply elsewhere, but who wants to go through the process again?

Marilyn Mosley has had great success at Laurel Springs School with finding apprenticeships for kids of all ages. She says:

Apprenticing is one of the best things you can do as a homeschooler. People who have great talent love to support homeschooled children and to share their wisdom with them. Mentors are available all over the world, and they come in all forms. Many, many people, whether you know them closely or not, will have an interest in mentoring a child if asked. I've spoken to people all over the country and just asked them to step in and work with a child, and it's phenomenal the number of people who do that because it fulfills their life purpose.

I've also directed families toward various organizations -- organizations even as large as NASA -- and some of the larger museums and universities. Children can access and participate in and become active in their programs. These places have graduate students who are interested in mentoring, and some institutions will even allow a child to apprentice from a distance. I have found that presenting the need to professionals all around the world has evoked in them a tremendous desire to help; everything from having children apprentice at a chimpanzee orphan farm in Zimbabwe to helping at a whale museum in Iceland. The resources in the world are phenomenal.

♥ Student Exchange Programs

Your child can become an exchange student for a year or more. The Council on International Educational Exchange (http://www.ciec.org/) can help your child find a friendly family to live with. This is a wonderful way for them to integrate, socialize and see how others live in different parts of the world.

♥ Travel

Travel is also a practical option that gives them the chance to experience the world in  ways that study can never accomplish. And it doesn't have to be expensive. If your child is willing to work as he goes, he can see the world. The Center for Interim Programs (http://www.interimprograms.com/) sends people to exotic places to do meaningful work, such as working in an orphanage in Jordan, teaching English on a faraway island, or helping out at a wildlife sanctuary.

As anyone knows who has visited other regions of the world or even other places in their own country, travel expands your mind by expanding your reference experiences beyond your own borders. You can gain great self-confidence, too, by being out in the world on your own. It could also expand your options -- whom you meet and the professional connections you can make.

♥ Trade School

For some students, trade schools are the ticket to getting the job they want in their field of interest. Learning specialized skills can give your child a cutting-edge education in a fraction of the time and for a fraction of the cost of college. Consider this option if your child already knows what he or she wants to do. It can be the beginning of a long, profitable career. Graduating from a trade school can give them an edge later when looking for work in that field, over others who do not have such thorough training. These include two- to four-year programs in the areas of:

Computer Programming   Mechanics
Arts—Graphic Design   Cosmetology
Entertainment industry   Nursing and more…
Broadcast journalism/video production

♥ The Military

The military can train your child to become a photographer, a journalist, or a translator—not just a soldier, sailor, or pilot. It's also not just for those looking for financial assistance for school. It's a great option for children who need to learn more discipline and/or a sense of responsibility, or who actually tend to do well with structure and discipline, teams, leadership, loyalty and a sense of mission.

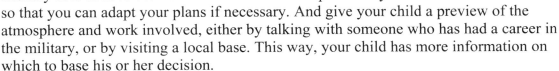

The caveat, however – besides the real possibility of having to go to war -- is that the military is not as homeschooling-friendly as it used to be. Be sure to research this option early on so that you can adapt your plans if necessary. And give your child a preview of the atmosphere and work involved, either by talking with someone who has had a career in the military, or by visiting a local base. This way, your child has more information on which to base his or her decision.

♥ Time Off

Your child could even benefit by taking time off before starting college. This will give your child a chance to see that there are lots of ways of expanding the mind that have nothing to do with school. Before your teen decides on a definite career path, have him or her spend some time watching and interviewing people who work in your child's field of interest. Your child can learn what the job is really like, and the interviews may prevent your child from spending time and money getting a degree for a job that may not be a good fit.

♥ Self-Employment/Entrepreneurship

Some kids have a natural proclivity to starting businesses. True business owners often are the ones who are willing to wake up early to deliver papers, mow lawns, hawk lemonade in your driveway or concoct some deal at a local bake sale that offers a better price or product than the competitor at the next table. You could probably predict their interest in going into business for themselves.

Becoming entrepreneurs is increasingly a choice young adults are making. Besides citing Bill Gates as a real role model, these is Richard Branson, who says that entrepreneurship "is the golden highway to economic freedom, plus it's an exciting and fun way to make a living." He also believes, "Being an entrepreneur is not only about making money. You can also tackle social problems with an entrepreneurial mind." He has even been knighted by the queen of England -- so try to stay open minded when your child enthusiastically says he wants to start his own business.

For some, entrepreneurship may seem like too big of a gamble, but a failed business does not mean your child has failed in the real world. While it's true that the majority of small businesses fail in the first few years, if your child's still living at home, and his new business goes under, nothing has really been lost and several things have been gained. If your child choose to work for a company later, the attempted business will still look great on the resume. And, if he still wants to try another startup, he can apply the lessons learned from any mistakes or reasons why the first one never got off the runway.

There's a lot to be said on this issue. Studies have shown that a full two-thirds of college students say they want to be entrepreneurs at some point in their lives. Consider that it might be better to do so sooner rather than later. Even if your child's business fails, at least his attempt will have been made before is married and has children or other responsibilities. Also, if your child decides to go to college after trying to start a business, he'll make better use of his time there. He will be heads above the average person, having already gleaned wisdom from experience.

Another benefit of owning a business is the creative freedom, flexibility and fulfillment it can provide. Too many people are working in jobs they don't like and that don't fulfill any particular gifts or dreams that they have. As homeschoolers, we teach our children that they can be successful at anything they set their minds to. They already have years of experience in developing their talents and interests. They're not exactly starting from scratch.

But can we raise them to be entrepreneurs? Wally Amos, of Famous Amos Cookies fame and fortune, says:

So many people want to start a business just so they can make a lot of money; that always seems to be the end result. But enjoying what you are doing is more important than making a lot of money. Now, it is important to have a business that is profitable, otherwise you cannot stay in business -- but it is more important for your child to follow his or her interests.

Entrepreneurs, I think, crop up early on. If you are watching your child, see what interests him or her and what he gravitates to. If you are an entrepreneur, then chances are your child is going to be one also, but not necessarily. None of my children are. I have one son who works with Boys and Girls Clubs, another son who works with a nonprofit group, another son who is interested in music, and a daughter who is interested in broadcast journalism. We are all different and you have to watch them and encourage them to do things they love to do.

♥ Prepare Them to Be Financially Responsible

Money and finances are particularly important topics because so many homeschooling families are living on one income while one parent stays home, at least part-time, with the children. We need good financial skills so that we can continue homeschooling our children without struggling. That's one of the nice things about homeschooling…we get to learn along with our children.

Maybe you have a list of skills you want your children to learn in addition to their curriculum – such as cooking, cleaning, or building. Please include on that skills list how to pay the bills, balance a checkbook, use a credit card and debit card wisely, balance a budget, and save and invest money. Talk about these skills with your child. This way you will be working "big picture backward" and they will be less likely to get lost or find themselves in debt along the way. These are important life skills that traditional education tends to overlook, as if children naturally spring into financially responsible and informed adults. The message we receive from the media is to consume. We are encouraged to spend, spend, spend. Very little is out there telling anyone to save before you spend. Credit card commercials make it look so fun and easy to enjoy the amenities of a luxurious lifestyle – "just charge it!" This is often the extent of kids' knowledge unless we parents provide a solid foundation of financial responsibility.

You can do this by teaching finances as its own subject, using any of the curriculum packages that are available. Or you can simply be a role model and involve them in how you run a household budget, how you choose investments, and how you make other financial decisions. If possible, ask the manager of your local bank if you can bring your children for a tour of the bank, with an explanation of its inner workings, and how checking and savings accounts work.

If you don't feel that managing your finances is your particular strong suit, then you'll benefit even more from this advice from Sharon Lechter, a life long education advocate and founder of Pay Your Family First and YOUTHpreneur.com, an innovative new way to spark the entrepreneurial spirit in our children. She is also co-author of *Think and Grow Rich - Three Feet from Gold*, the international bestselling book *Rich Dad Poor Dad* and many of the Rich Dad books and products. As a member of the President's Advisory Council on Financial Literacy, Sharon helps shape the state of financial literacy in our nation along with 18 other members selectively appointed by President Bush. Sharon has been a pioneer in developing new technologies to bring education into children's lives in ways that are challenging and fun. Here are some of the things Sharon Lechter told me in an interview I did for Homeschool.com called "Give Your Children a Financial Head Start."

Many of our educational systems don't look at money as a part of life. We need to teach our children that it is, because the world they are going to face is very different from the world that we, as parents, faced.

The concept of YOUTHpreneur *and all the books and products we develop is to get people through the fear of money so that they can take more control over their life and more control over their financial education. Certainly for parents, my goal is to provide them with the tools to help train their children early, so those kids have a chance to really create the future they want.*

A majority of our high school students are graduating from high school already with credit card debt. Our college students are graduating $22,000 in debt because we are allowing them to learn from television, the Internet, and their peers how to spend money. I get furious when freshman in college go to school and they literally walk a gauntlet of tables when they are arriving at college the first day with people handing out CD players and water bottles – if they just sign up for a credit card. It's not the credit card or the ATM card that's the problem. It's the lack of education that goes with it. Our children are going to be in a world where everybody has credit cards. You can't rent a car or get a hotel room without having a credit card. There are lots of cards out there that have guaranteed balances; there are lots of credit cards that let the parents have a string account so that they can see what is happening. It's through that inner play between the parents and the children that you can help instruct them on how to utilize a credit card wisely.

I have a lot of credit cards, but I've never paid any interest on my credit cards because I pay them off every month. I love them; they help me keep my books straight.

There are three basic types of income. One is earned, and that's you working for money, that's your paycheck, your W2, your 1099. That's earned income and that also happens to be the most highly taxed income.

Then you have passive income such as what you would earn from royalties. A majority of passive income is from real estate investments. Then there is portfolio income -- income from paper assets. With passive income, you could build a business or buy a franchise, where you are not physically there every day but the business system is working for you. So you are getting income from this business without you necessarily having to be there.

I often get asked how early, how young is too young, to be teaching children about money. My reply is, At what age do you think a child recognizes the difference between a one-dollar bill and a twenty-dollar bill?

It's a wonderful self esteem builder for children to earn something before they can buy it. Experiential learning is key and is the basis of all our YOUTHpreneur programs and products. We have had kids ask their parents to buy them a bubble-gum machine and they've put them out in local businesses. It's keeping the concept of understanding the difference between assets and liabilities. It's something that you can start at a very early age -- gumball machines are just one small example. We've got children who are creating websites for other people. Other kids get together and they provide babysitting or tutoring services for other families. A young man that I know started mowing lawns, and then all of a sudden he got his friends involved, so now he doesn't mow any lawns anymore. He is the business founder and has a group of 10 children that work for him mowing lawns.

Being an entrepreneur is using that creativity to create business, to create jobs, and to continue to support the economy through new and novel ideas. Having an entrepreneurial spirit is not a requirement. It is something we all have. What happens is we get trained out of it, we have fear taught through school, and we become employees who just follow the rules. School teaches us that there is only one right answer. I think everyone would agree that once you get out of school, you find out that there are a lot of right answers and there are a lot of wrong answers.

The goal is to keep our children excited about learning, and excited about being creative, so that they have the opportunity to create the life they want.

If you are giving your kids allowance when they think of extra things they can do, then you are actually inspiring them in the entrepreneurial spirit. If they say, "Mom, I did the dishes, but how about I clean out the cabinets?" They are the ones thinking of things they can do for extra money. That kind of allowance inspires entrepreneurism. But if they just know that each and every week they are going to get $10 whether they watch TV or make their bed, this instills the employee mentality. I really believe that parents can take control and help instill in their children this concept of earning money, being creative, and finding new ways to make money. Let them think of something that they want and help them save the money and be able to go get it as a celebration for the fact that they wanted it, they waited for it, they earned it, and then they bought it. They didn't borrow money to get it.

For more information regarding Sharon Lechter, Pay Your Family First, LLC or YOUTHpreneur programs, please visit YOUTHpreneur.com or email info@youthpreneur.com.

CHAPTER TEN

PUTTING IT ALL TOGETHER
A Footpath to the Future

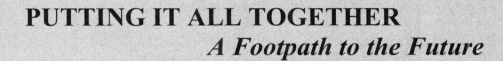

♥ **Get Inspired!**

♥ **Help Your Kids Fill In Their Custom Home Learning Plan**

♥ **Empower Your Children With the 8 Keys to Lifelong Success**

Congratulations—you've made it through all the necessary steps to becoming a top-notch homeschooler. You're now ready to have your best year ever. You can use this same template every year of your children's homeschooling to give them each a quality education, from their toddler years right through to their teen years and beyond. If you haven't yet filled in your Custom Home Learning Plan, that's fine too. You can just go back through the instructions for the exercises within each chapter and fill it out now. Your Custom Home Learning Plan will serve as your template for each semester, helping you stay on top of your homeschooling. In this final chapter, I will show you ways that you and your children can continue staying motivated and successful, even beyond homeschooling and into college and the real world.

♥ 8 Keys to Your Children's Future Success and Happiness

Bobbi DePorter is the creator of SuperCamp, a residential summer program for kids designed to teach students academic and personal skills in an environment fostering self-esteem and confidence and operated on college campuses across the country. She's also the Founder of the Quantum Learning Network Training for teachers, administrators and students in 30 states. She's written seven books published in seven languages.

According to DePorter, there are three factors that work together to create an effective, confident, motivated lifelong learner and achiever:

> 1) Your mindset
> 2) Knowing your learning styles
> 3) Applying specific learning strategies to understand anything.

Excellence and success come from the following eight qualities, attitudes and habits. These are the qualities we want to foster—and teaching by example, of course -- throughout our children's education:

The 8 Keys to Success
> 1. Integrity
> 2. Knowing that "Failure leads to success"
> 3. Speaking with positive purpose and intention
> 4. Having a "This is it" attitude; being present now
> 5. Commitment
> 6. Ownership
> 7. Flexibility
> 8. Balance

In an interview with Homeschool.com, Bobbi DePorter explained each attribute in more detail.

What is a Quantum Learner? For us it's someone who has a certain mindset. This person says, "I am responsible for my life. I have skills for academic excellence and I'm motivated and confident. I love to learn. I expect great results. I know my learning styles. I think creatively. I set goals. I've got these strategies that I can apply and I picture myself successful."

There is a difference between motivation and discipline. Both are important. Motivation is doing what needs to be done when it needs to be done because you want to do it. Discipline is doing what needs to be done when it needs to be done, even when you don't want to do it.

*The first of the 8 keys of excellence is **integrity**. Integrity is having your values match your behaviors and actions. First you need to discover of all discover what you value, and then match your actions to that. When they are congruent, then we are in integrity, and we always say that these are values of moral excellence.*

*The next one is knowing that **failure leads to success**. It's so powerful to reframe our mistakes into gifts of what we can learn from them. We have what are called gems and opportunities. Gems are the feedback from "What did you do well?" Opportunities are the feedback from "What can we do better?" We learn to get excited about our gems and opportunities so that our failures can lead to success.*

*The third key is **speaking with good purpose**, which is controlling the intention of our words. We don't have to say everything we think, but when we do, the intention of our words should always be to build people up. So when I have something I want to tell somebody, I always stop and think, "Will that build them up? Will that build our relationship up?" and "How is it serving?"*

*The fourth key to success is thinking **this is it!** – which means making the most of every moment and living in the present time. When we talk to students, they could say, "Oh, I'm studying math and I don't like it. I wish I was with my friends at the mall or on the beach, anything but this." Their mind is wandering someplace else. With a "this is it" attitude, whether it's math class or studying, whatever you are doing, give it your all. "This is it. What can I do to make the most of it?"*

*The next success key is **ownership**, and that means taking responsibility -- being accountable for all your actions and what you've accomplished both good and bad. When you've made a mistake and somebody is trying to lay blame or put it on someone else or give excuses, there is no ownership in that. When you've made a mistake, take full ownership. I always picture in my mind stepping right into things, stepping forward, stepping into it and saying, "I need to do it differently, I did these things and what can I do to make it right?" People respect that… Power is taking ownership. We also talk about students taking ownership of their education, of their learning, of everything in their life.*

*Key number seven is **flexibility**, which is changing what we need to do to get to our goal. Flexibility being willing to change a strategy. If something is not working, try something else. Keep what's working and let go of what's not working…*

*The final key to success is achieving **balance**. Balance is doing things that are fulfilling in life. When you are doing something that is really meaningful, having that commitment and doing things that make a difference for others, you will have that sense of fulfillment that brings balance to your life. When you know you are living your best life or being your best self, you are working on yourself, you are being a lifelong learner, you are doing what brings joy and happiness…that's balance."*

Her words are so valuable—just endeavoring to put these eight principles into practice is a lifelong education in itself!

The mindset of success can carry kids forward and stay with them their whole lives, making them more confident and happier overall. It empowers them to be themselves.

♥ The Secrets to Staying Inspired

Inspiration is the best motivation. Here's how to stay inspired:
- Remember the bigger picture
- Have more fun
- Fulfill a sense of purpose by being of service and making a contribution
- Build confidence with a track record of successes
- Celebrate

♥   Remember the Bigger Picture

If you ever feel mired in the details of your curriculum schedule or if your child starts losing interest in the day-to-day work, remember the long-term vision, the reason why you do what you do. "Seeing the bigger picture" could mean keeping your eyes on the prize, seeing you and your child living the life they you both are only dreaming of now. Or it could mean simply seeing all there is to be grateful for. That's a very big picture indeed.

We need reminders, often every day, to have fun and enjoy what we do and to appreciate that we are giving a wonderful gift by homeschooling our children.

The bigger picture for so many parents is getting their children into a fantastic college, or watching them grow to enjoy a happy, healthy, successful life. Some of us don't like to imagine the future, when our children will have flown the coop. The reality is, however, our children are forever moving onward and upward. And so are you! If your motivation is waning, perhaps you've forgotten that. Each of us has the opportunity to change and grow and make new choices every single day of our lives. I hope you have come to believe that you too are always capable of learning new things, and accomplishing more than you might have ever thought possible.

If you ever feel off-track or your child is balking at a lesson plan, try these strategies:

- Refer to your Family on a Mission statement.
- Look at your child's goal list. Have your child write a few more goals.
- Allow some time to daydream. Your child's energy and creativity will come back.
- Remind your child of his or her strengths and learning style.
- Make sure the curriculum relates in some way to the fulfillment of your child's overall plans and interests.

What inspires you? What inspires your child? Make room for those things in your lives. This will get your child excited again about his or her studies because it relates to who your child is and who your child wants to become. **These are all related to the big picture – *the eternal things of life.***

❤ Have More Fun

One homeschooling mom confessed that she told her children, "I'm gonna flag down for you the first school bus that goes by—I don't even care what school it's going to!" This feeling is often called burnout and it's real. Anecdotal evidence suggests that burnout is most likely to occur when a family is trying to do too much, trying to do too well, trying to duplicate public schools, or trying to do all of the above. Don't let burnout ruin a good thing. Drop what you're doing and get outside! If homeschooling is becoming like bitter medicine for both of you or like a trudge up a never-ending hill, something's missing -- oh yeah! The joy of learning. Get it back!

**While it's good to keep the end goals in mind,
it's also important to simply enjoy each day along the way.**

I have interviewed over 32 of the top homeschooling and education experts in the country, and they all say the same thing: Homeschooling your children should be fun, and raising your children should be fun.

I honestly think people are sometimes afraid of fun. They think having fun is frivolous. We receive these messages in society, the keep-your-nose-to-the-grindstone approach, the Puritan work ethic, a school of hard knocks attitude, and believe that something has to be really hard in order for it be valuable. If it comes too easily, or if you have "too much fun" doing it, then it must not really count.

I hope you don't believe that anymore. This semester is going to be joyful and fun and rewarding. And have no doubt, a LOT of learning is going to be take place -- meaningful learning that will be remembered forever. And your children are going to be learning and practicing a system for living that they can use forever.

If your homeschooling hits a snag, do the following:

✓ Check to see if you've fallen into a boring routine. If so, take the kids on a surprise field trip to the zoo or the beach, let them stay up later, or make it a "snow day" and ask them what they want to play!

✓ Instead of book learning…Do a science experiment such as looking at things under a microscope, bring in a dance instructor for a family swing dance lesson, or build a jungle gym together in the backyard.

✓ Do something you've never done before, or something totally outrageous; Stage a play for your neighbors, Make it Silly Costume Day, Have a Karaoke Night. Do something you'll remember for a long time! (And videotape it for family fun night years later.)

♥ **Fulfill a Sense of Purpose and Contribution or Service**

Sometimes it's just good to get out of your own way, stop thinking about what you need, and do something for someone else. When we focus too much on ourselves, or "get caught up in the rat race," we need to remind ourselves what gives us true fulfillment. Most of the time this involves giving service and making a difference in someone else's life.

**Don't let memories from your own school days about what education is supposed to look like override what your current experience reveals to you.
Listen to your heart.**

• Have everyone in the house round up the clothes, toys and books they're not using, put them in bags and take a trip to your local Salvation Army, women's shelter or homeless family shelter.

• Help your kids organize a fund-drive for a local cause.

• This may be ambitious, but take in a foreign exchange student. It will teach your kids about another culture, and at the same time help out someone else's child.

• Become a part of your neighborhood or state homeschoolers' group and offer others guidance and direction. Share experiences and resources and arrange multi-family field trips.

Volunteering, contributing, donating…these all make us feel we are an integral part of a larger community. We need each other. Homeschooling parents get immeasurable personal rewards from being role models for others and from making newcomers feel a part of their special group.

Doing service teaches kids so many priceless lessons to kids about the world and their important role in it. This is especially true if they lack confidence—helping others reminds them they are significant and special. It makes their education relevant, so they can get excited about learning all over again.

♥ Build Confidence and Keep a Track Record of Successes

Low self-esteem is a terrible problem for youth of today. Filling out the Custom Home Learning Plan gives you a chance to guide their progress, and at the same time you're acknowledging their abilities and preferences. Over time, they will be able to look back and see all they have accomplished. This can become an important, confidence-building document for them.

Homeschooled kids don't always realize all of the learning that they are doing because they don't receive report cards or progress reports. Keep your Custom Home Learning Plan as a record of your children's many <u>achievements</u>.

Sometimes lack of confidence can be the result of self-doubt. Perhaps you haven't accomplished half of your plans; you just know that other homeschoolers are doing a much better job; your children aren't even close to that image of perfection you imagined they would reach through homeschooling.

Homeschooling is much more than school at home. The lessons your child learns from just being around you are just as, or more important than academics. The big picture grows clearer, giving you the ability to put the curriculum, books, and tests into perspective. If you continue observing your children and experimenting with educational approaches, and if you continue your own education about homeschooling, then you will grow to trust yourself and your children more.

"Getting real" about homeschooling is liberating. You open new paths to learning that you didn't know existed before, and one day your child will thank you for it.

Remember…

❤ Don't waste time second-guessing yourself. There will always be something you wish you had done differently, or didn't do, or did instead. It's much more productive to spend your time using what you have discovered to guide future decisions.

❤ Never compare yourself or your children to others. Checking that you and your child have moved forward from where you started is a more accurate and useful gauge of your success.

❤ Remind your children when they have completed a semester or year goal. Find a way to celebrate it with something they like…another glow-in-the-dark star on their ceiling, make a public announcement at dinner.

❤ As a parent and teacher who also works and plays, start a journal of the positive homeschooling experiences you've had. Remind yourself of everything that's right in your life.

Celebrate!

In finishing this *Homeschooling and Loving It!* book, your children will have learned an invaluable skill set: how to set a goal, achieve it, and celebrate. Ideally, setting a vision and then following through with a plan to achieve that vision will become a habit for life. And celebrating is the icing on the cake.

If you are feeling a need to lighten up, then you're joining countless other homeschoolers who report that this is normal and beneficial. When you worry less and focus more on what you have accomplished, it becomes easier to relax and enjoy the ride.

Start by celebrating your child's completion of his or her Custom Home Learning Plan. One of the best ways to celebrate this is to take a photo each time a goal is reached. Then attach the photos to the plan and tape them to the refrigerator. You can also staple written work samples to the Learning Plan – perhaps a report or story or poem that your child is really proud of, or even "before and after" samples of handwriting. It can be anything you or your child wants.

Building a track record of success is a huge confidence builder. Your children will begin to set bigger and bigger goals, knowing that they have a way to follow through and reach them.

- Have random celebrations, sometimes for no reason at all. Instead of getting rewarded only for accomplishments, they deserve a party just for being themselves.
- Hug your child. It's easy to get busy and forget this simple act.
- Spice things up with a spice cake baking contest in the middle of the day.
- Congratulate them on working so hard. Announce that you're all playing hookey together that day, and in honor of who they are, they get to choose what they want to do that day or where they want to go.
- Arrange a surprise party for the end of the school year. Have your child blow out a candle for each goal she reached that year!

♥ The Final Step: Putting It All Together

Now it's time to complete a **CUSTOM HOME LEARNING PLAN** for each of your children. This will be your footpath to the future.

Be sure to take photos as you go along and tape or glue them to the photo spots in the Plan. This way your Plan will also serve as a meaningful portfolio of all the wonderful things you do in your homeschool.

We have come to the end of this book. But it is just the start of your journey into your best homeschooling year ever.

I have given you tips, techniques, excerpts and encouragement. I have offered you ways to discover your child's learning style and your personal teaching style. I have shared methods and inspiration so that you can de-clutter and organize your curriculum and supplies, your valuable time, and your learning environment. Now it is up to you to employ them in your own rich and unique life, reflecting the style of your family.

The following **Custom Home Learning Plan** is designed for making multiple copies so that you can have one for each of your children. This Plan gives you space in which you can write your goals, hopes and dreams. It also provides a way to document meeting and exceeding those hopes and dreams in photographs.

Please feel free to contact me by email at Rebecca@Homeschool.com. I'd love to hear how this book is working for you. Continue with your unlimited hope for your children and yourself....as you continue Homeschooling and Loving It!

Wishing you all the best,

Rebecca Kochenderfer

Editor in Chief
Homeschool.com

YOUR CUSTOM HOME LEARNING PLAN

- ♥ Make a copy for each of your children.
- ♥ Fill in the blanks.
- ♥ Put this Plan on a wall somewhere so that you can see it every day.
- ♥ Take a photo and tape or glue it to the Plan every time a goal is achieved.
- ♥ Save these pages for your permanent portfolio. Your children will love to look back on all they have accomplished.

My Custom Home Learning Plan

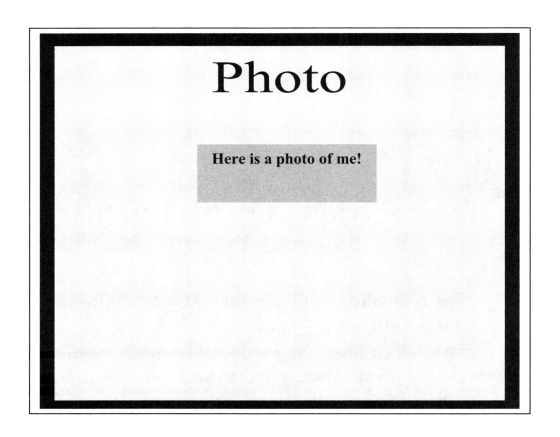

_____

(Name)

_____

(Date)

Q: What do you want to be, do or have "when you grow up"? What do you think you would like to do for your career?
A:

_____
_____
_____
_____

Q: Do you want to go to college? If so, is there some college(s) in particular you would like to attend?
A:

_____
_____
_____
_____

Q: Do you have an interest in starting your own business? If so, what type of business?
A:

_____
_____
_____
_____

Q: Is there anything special you want to know how to do before you leave home and move out on your own?
A:

_____
_____
_____
_____

Q: What is your #1 goal for this semester or year?

My #1 goal is to:

_____
_____
_____
_____

> # Photo
>
> **Here is a photo of me
> reaching my goal!**

Q: How you are planning to achieve this particular goal?
A:_____
_____
_____
_____

Q: Do you have any other big goals you want to work on for this semester or year?
A:_____
_____

Specific goals for each subject area

Q: What do you want to learn or do for Math?

A:_____

_____

_____

Photo

Photo achieving your Math goal.

Perhaps with a math book you have finished
or a photo of your test with an "A" on it.
What type of photo will work best for you?

Q: What is your goal for Reading?

A:_____

_____

_____

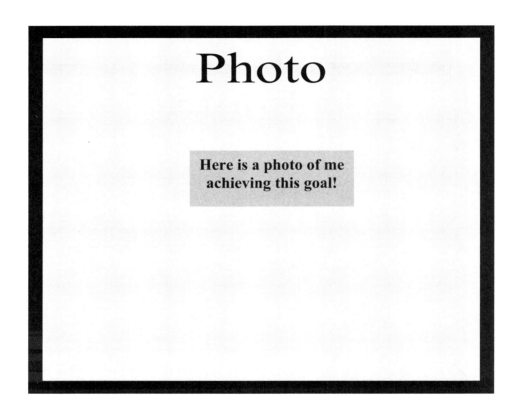

Perhaps a photo of you surrounded by all of the books you have read.
What type of photo shows how you achieved your reading goal?

Q: What is your goal for Science?

A:_____

_____

_____

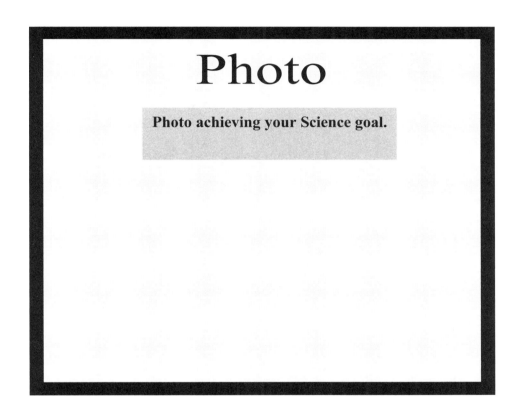

Perhaps a photo of you conducting a science experiment.
Or a photo of your science fair project. You choose!

Q: What is your goal for History?

A:_____

_____

_____

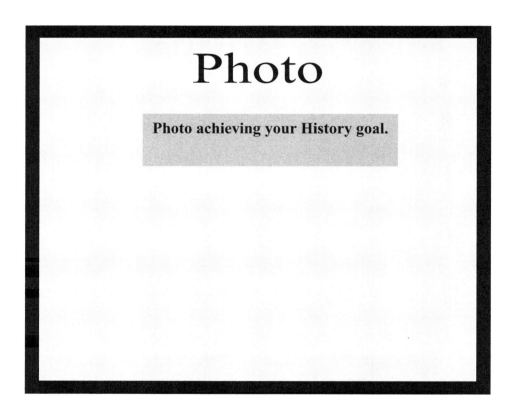

Photo achieving your History goal.

Q: What is your goal for Writing?

A:_____

_____

_____

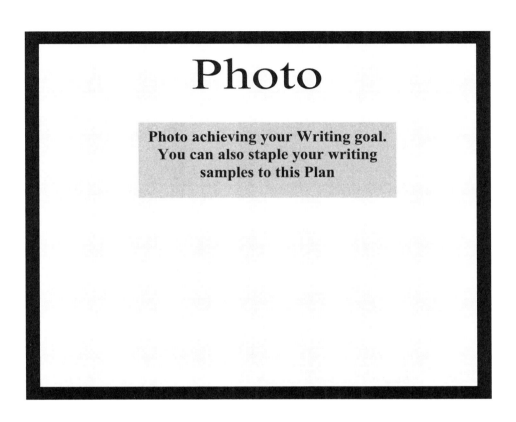

Photo

**Photo achieving your Writing goal.
You can also staple your writing
samples to this Plan**

Q: Do you have any special goals for fitness, music, art or foreign language(s)?

A:_____
_____
_____
_____
_____

Photo achieving your goal.

Photo achieving your goal.

Photo achieving your goal.

Q: What goals would your parents like to add?

A:

1. _____
2. _____
3. _____

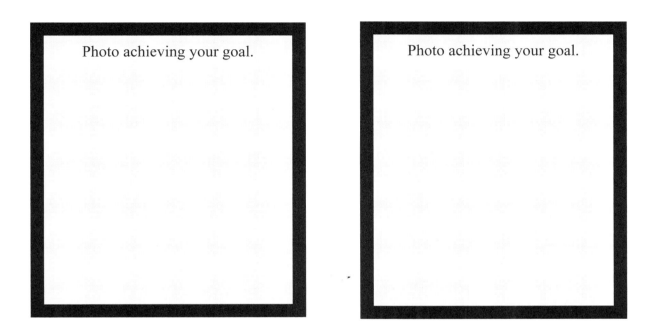

Photo achieving your goal.

Photo achieving your goal.

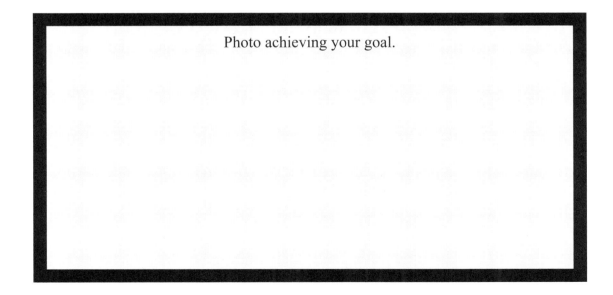

Photo achieving your goal.

What is your learning style?

Q: Do you know what your dominant learning modality is? Do you learn better by reading, listening, or touching? (If you are not sure, you can take a free quick quiz at www.howtolearn.com or you can answer the quiz in chapter four of *Homeschooling and Loving It!*.)

A._____

_____

Q: What is your learning personality? (Circle the one that best describes you.)

I am a Performer. I like to move. I crave variety. I am a risk taker. I am competitive and I like having an audience. I am good with my hands.

I am a Producer/Planner. I think logically and am orderly. I like workbooks and structure. I like to plan things out.

I am an Inventor. I ask lots of questions. I am a builder and I learn by making connections.

I am an Inspirer. I like win-win relationships. I am caring and sensitive. I like harmony and working in teams.

I am a Thinking/Creative person. I may become an artist, musician or writer. I am a deep thinker.

Q: There are lots of different types of "smart". If you want, you can take a free "multiple intelligences" quiz at www.davidlazear.com. What type of smart are you? Word smart, body smart, people smart, self smart, nature smart, math smart, visual smart, music smart?

A: According to the quiz, I am particularly _____smart. This makes sense to me because I tend to be good at...

_____

Q: Can you name 5 of your strengths? What are you really good at? These can be anything -- for example, traveling, writing, being optimistic, teaching....you name it!

A: 1. _____

       2. _____

       3. _____

       4. _____

       5. _____

Next, list your 100 Before-I-Die Goals. What do you want to do, be, see, have or learn? (List as many as you can.)

_____   _____
_____   _____
_____   _____
_____   _____
_____   _____
_____   _____
_____   _____
_____   _____
_____   _____
_____   _____
_____   _____
_____   _____
_____   _____
_____   _____
_____   _____
_____   _____
_____   _____
_____   _____
_____   _____
_____   _____
_____   _____
_____   _____
_____   _____
_____   _____
_____   _____
_____   _____
_____   _____
_____   _____
_____   _____
_____   _____
_____   _____

Where and when do you study best?

Q. Where do you work best? Where do you do your best studying?
(For example, at the table, on your bed, or in front of the TV.)
Do you prefer quiet? Or do you like to have music or sound around you?

A._____
_____

Q: When do you think best? Do you do your best studying in the

1. Morning
2. Afternoon
3. Evening

Here's the key. Remember to set yourself up for success by using your special abilities and interests to their fullest. This is what makes you unique. This is how you let yourself shine!

Q: You have to know how to take good care of yourself and pace yourself. How do you like to relax and recharge? Is it by reading quietly? Watching a movie? Talking on the phone with friends? How can you avoid stress and make sure you are relaxed and energetic?

A:_____
_____
_____
_____
_____

Special questions for high school students

Q: What classes have you already taken? Which classes do you need for your diploma? For college? For your career?

A: You may want to chart this out. To find out your state's diploma requirements, you can do an Internet search for the name of your state or province plus "diploma requirement." Then go to your college web site and find out its requirements. Most colleges require four years each of math, science, history, and English. They are also looking for 200 hours of volunteer hours.

Check off your total years.

Subject/Year	1 year	2 years	3 years	4 years
English				
History				
Math				
Science				

Q: What tests will you need to take? Be sure to plan ahead for the high school exit exam, the PSAT, and the SAT or ACT. Remember, you can take the SAT/ACT two to three times to get your highest score.

PSAT date: _____

ACT date: _____

SAT date: _____

AP Exam dates: _____

Other test dates:

Test name   Date

_____   _____

_____   _____

_____   _____

_____   _____

Notes for any other special dates:

LAUREL SPRINGS™
COLLEGE PREPARATORY DISTANCE LEARNING

Laurel Springs School, a college preparatory distance learning school, is offering these scholarships to readers of Homeschooling and Loving It.

www.LaurelSprings.com   (800) 377-5890

Home Schooling families believe a purposeful life is part of the learning process.

At Laurel Springs, we believe actualizing one's dreams is the purpose of education. We encourage students to explore their deepest held hopes and dreams and demonstrate them through core academic subjects, dance, drama, athletics, technology, travel, language, art and more. Contact an Enrollment Advisor and develop an academic plan that will lead to acceptance into the college of your choice.

scholarships

$250 Grades K-7th   **$300** Grades 8th-12th

LAUREL SPRINGS™ COLLEGE PREPARATORY DISTANCE LEARNING

Actualize your mission and vision of reaching your child's education and life goals.

Contact an Enrollment Advisor who will develop an academic plan that will lead to acceptance to the college of your child's choice. Call to enroll in Laurel Springs School.

scholarship

$300 Grades 8th-12th

LAUREL SPRINGS™ COLLEGE PREPARATORY DISTANCE LEARNING

Put in place a step-by-step plan to actualize your family mission.

You and your LSS teacher will work together to understand the unique way your child learns best, enhancing your child's special way of learning. An LSS Student Services Advisor will evaluate your student's transcript to determine the courses needed to stay on track.

scholarships

$250 Grades K-7th   **$300** Grades 8th-12th

LAUREL SPRINGS™ COLLEGE PREPARATORY DISTANCE LEARNING

Enroll now to receive your scholarship!

Call (800) 377-5890 or visit www.LaurelSprings.com

One offer per student applied to a full time enrollment in Laurel Springs School. These scholarship offers may not be applied in conjunction with other scholarships or financial aid.

Enroll now to receive your scholarship!

Call (800) 377-5890 or visit www.LaurelSprings.com

One offer per student applied to a full time enrollment in Laurel Springs School. These scholarship offers may not be applied in conjunction with other scholarships or financial aid.

Enroll now to receive your scholarship!

Call (800) 377-5890 or visit www.LaurelSprings.com

One offer per student applied to a full time enrollment in Laurel Springs School. These scholarship offers may not be applied in conjunction with other scholarships or financial aid.

Enroll now to receive your scholarship!

Call (800) 377-5890 or visit www.LaurelSprings.com

One offer per student applied to a full time enrollment in Laurel Springs School. These scholarship offers may not be applied in conjunction with other scholarships or financial aid.

The Mastery-based method of education allows for a win/win approach to learning.

LSS has a student-centered, mastery-based program that nurtures and supports your child's dreams. We do not believe in "lose." We believe the school and parents win when your child wins. Our unique program applies the mastery-based courses, including our prestigious college-prep, Honors and advanced placement courses.

·············· scholarships ··············

$250 Grades K-7th $300 Grades 8th-12th

Understanding your child's unique learning style provides for academic and personal success.

At Laurel Springs, we understand your child's unique learning style. This understanding enhances your child's passion for learning. We can personalize our teaching method and curriculum to match your child's unique style of learning. We ensure the model matches the child, rather than the child matching the model.

·············· scholarships ··············

$250 Grades K-7th $300 Grades 8th-12th

Collaborating and celebrating differences makes it possible for 1+1 to equal 3.

When we leverage our unique differences, using a collaborative method, the whole becomes greater than the sum of its parts. If your child qualifies and is accepted into Laurel Springs Academy for the Gifted and Talented, we will provide a scholarship or financial aid.

Applicable to Laurel Springs Academy for the Gifted and Talented.

·············· scholarship ··············

$1,000 Grades 8th-12th

Homeschooling allows you to create a balanced approach that supports and nurtures the whole child. Take time for renewal of the physical, mental, social, and spiritual dimensions.

Kids4Earth is a seventh grade environmental science course that supports an understanding of your child's relationship with the environment and gives him the opportunity to become actively involved in making a difference. Also, our high school elective portfolios provide course credit so your child can pursue his interests, passions and dreams.

·············· scholarships ··············

$300 Grade 7th Kids4Earth Course $300 Grades 9th-12th Elective Portfolio

Enroll now to receive your scholarship!

Call (800) 377-5890 or visit <u>www.LaurelSprings.com</u>

One offer per student applied to a full time enrollment in Laurel Springs School. These scholarship offers may not be applied in conjunction with other scholarships or financial aid.

Enroll now to receive your scholarship!

Call (800) 377-5890 or visit <u>www.LaurelSprings.com</u>

One offer per student applied to a full time enrollment in Laurel Springs School. These scholarship offers may not be applied in conjunction with other scholarships or financial aid.

A DIVISION OF LAUREL SPRINGS SCHOOL

Enroll now to receive your scholarship!

Call (800) 377-5890 or visit <u>www.LSAGiftedandTalented.com</u>

One offer per student applied to a full time enrollment in Laurel Springs Academy. These scholarship offers may not be applied in conjunction with other scholarships or financial aid.

Enroll now to receive your scholarship!

Call (800) 377-5890 or visit <u>www.LaurelSprings.com</u>

One offer per student applied to a full time enrollment in Laurel Springs School. These scholarship offers may not be applied in conjunction with other scholarships or financial aid.